SAINT LOUIS TEMPLE

BOOK *of* REMEMBRANCE

nineteen hundred ninety-seven

SAINT LOUIS TEMPLE

BOOK *of* REMEMBRANCE

Second Edition 2017

The original edition of this book was published in 1997 for inclusion in the materials placed in the cornerstone of the temple at the time of its dedication. Additional copies were produced for stake presidents in the temple district and a few for retention by the temple.

The twentieth-year celebration of the temple dedication resulted in many requests for copies of the book. Thus, this edition of the book has been made available, at printer's cost, through *Celestialife LLC*, a not-for-profit entity. The soft-cover, print-on-demand format enables the lowest possible cost for readers.

It is hoped that this new edition will provide great enjoyment to those who wish to know of the remarkable events that resulted in the creation of this beautiful House of the Lord and of its enthusiastic acceptance by the entire Saint Louis community.

This second edition of:
SAINT LOUIS TEMPLE
is available through:
Amazon.com
BarnesandNoble.com
Booksamillion.com

table of contents

ACKNOWLEDGEMENTS

*T*his book provides an account of the beginnings, the construction and dedication of the Saint Louis Missouri Temple. It identifies some but by no means all of those who have had a part in bringing this 50th Temple of the Lord Jesus Christ to reality in these latter-days. In particular the hand of the Lord Himself is acknowledged in making this temple as well as all things possible.

It has been a special privilege to be involved in the preparation and publishing of this book. Those whose unique and creative skills and remarkable energies have contributed to it include the following as well as numerous others without whose help this publication would not have been accomplished:

DESIGN AND PRODUCTION
Paul Jarvis • Tanya Jarvis • Courtney Walker

EDITING
Robert Goodrich • Teresa Hirst

The completion of a temple in St. Louis has been a long sought dream for thousands of Latter-day Saints for many years. The realization of this dreams has required the faith, dedication, energy and vision of additional thousands, including the early pioneers who sacrificed so much, including for many their lives; those who struggled to keep the church alive through the lean years between the departure of the body of Saints in the early 1800s and the time of the re-energizing of the church in the mid 1900s; those faithful and dedicated leaders who brought the church to stakehood and then multiplied those stakes including Roy Oscarson, Boyd Schenk, Mardean Steinmetz, Vern Stromberg, Grant Rees and so many others who either migrated to St. Louis or joined the church as converts, thus swelling the ranks and providing the mass required to justify a temple in this part of the kingdom. The list is endless.

An additional list need also be complied of faithful who have planned, worked, sweat, shivered, and sacrificed to accomplish all that has been necessary to obtain the land, secure the necessary permits for development and construction, present and promote the project favorably with the public, implement the groundbreaking ceremony, to accomplish the design, construction and finally to actually open the temple, the dedication and cornerstone ceremonies. Only the omniscient could truly count all who have contributed.

For my part it has been an extraordinary privilege to be involved in this project beginning with the acquisition of the land and culminating in the call from President Hinckley inviting me and Mary Jean to serve as the first president and matron of the temple. I cannot adequately express the profound admiration and gratitude I have for the dedicated members of the St. Louis Temple Committee who are named elsewhere in this book. Their accomplishments have been at times miraculous and their talents amazing. And throughout, their spirit has been indomitable, often enabling them to surmount the insurmountable... all done with good grace, wit and love for one another. Even magnificent seems inadequate to describe them and their accomplishments.

Other without whom none of this would have been possible include Derek Metcalfe, Manger of the Temple Department whose steady hand, keen perceptions and profound knowledge have been indispensible...John Hardy who has worked beside Brother Metcalfe and has given constant support...Gary Holland who has overseen construction with his keen competence and warm easy demeanor...Bruce Olsen, Director of Public Affairs for the Church who has overseen the very successful efforts in this area...Elder Hugh W. Pinnock and the other Area Presidents who have given direction and support in so many ways as has Elder Eugene Hansen, Executive Director of the Temple Department. We must all acknowledge the vision and leadership of President Gordon B. Hinckley whose special interest in St. Louis and this temple have been crucial in bringing the temple to reality. Finally and above all, the praise and glory go to our Lord Jesus Christ without whom neither this temple nor any good or worthwhile thing would be possible. To all I express my deepest thanks, love and respect.

Gratefully,

Menlo F. Smith
Vice Chairman, St. Louis Temple Committee

ST. LOUIS MISSOURI TEMPLE

one • SITE ACQUISITION

The following account contains details explaining the temple site acquisition, the temple task committee and the project hearings. Through the forementioned process, there was no public opposition and we acknowledge the Lord's hand in the outcome of the St. Louis Temple.

JUNE 1989

Brother Clair Bankhead of the Temples and Special Projects Department at Church Headquarters called Menlo F. Smith, then serving as Regional Representative, informing him confidentially that plans were being made to build a temple in St. Louis. He was requested to work with Harry Hays, Vice President of Gundaker Realty Commercial Group, to locate and acquire a suitable site. Five possible sites were identified and evaluated. A presentation depicting these sites was forwarded to Salt Lake City for review. Shortly afterward word was received that President Gordon B. Hinckley, Counselor in the First Presidency, would be coming to St. Louis to review the possible sites.

JUNE 23, 1989

Call received by Menlo Smith from President Hinckley advising that he would be in St. Louis on the following Sunday. He requested that his visit not be announced but that he be taken to visit the five sites shown in the presentation from which two would be selected to show to President Thomas S. Monson at 5pm on Sunday, June 25 and shown to President Ezra Taft Benson on Monday, June 26.

June 25, 1989

President Hinckley and Menlo Smith visited each of the five possible sites. Knowing that he would be more favorably impressed with the site adjacent to the Missouri Baptist College, that was shown to him last. Immediately upon seeing it, he asked, "Can this site be purchased?" He was informed that it was listed for sale but that it would require approval by the Missouri Baptist College Board of Trustees and that would be problematic. He instructed Brother Smith to proceed to determine whether or not purchase could be effected.

At 5pm Menlo Smith took President Monson to show him the two sites which were most favored. He readily agreed with President Hinckley's preference.

June 26, 1989

President Benson was taken to see the two preferred sites. He also readily agreed with President Hinckley's selection. While President Benson was partially invalid at this time and had less than full use of faculties, there was no doubt in his mind as to which was the preferred site.

The preferred site was being offered for sale by a developer, Love Properties. Love had purchased the 19 acre site some years prior from the Missouri Baptist College which had held it up to that time for possible future expansion of their college campus. While Love held title to the property, it was evidently stipulated in their purchase agreement that if they did not develop the property and chose to sell it, that such sale would require approval by the college Board of Trustees. Because certain segments of the Baptist Church have been quite persistent in objecting to our temples, it seemed highly uncertain as to whether purchase of this property would be possible.

June 28, 1989

The site being offered consisted of 19 acres fronting on North Forty Drive overlooking Highway 40. The east end of the property drops deeply into a flood plain and was thus not useful for building. Just west of the drop off is a drive providing access from North Outer Forty Drive to the college campus. Menlo Smith requested that Harry Hays determine the following:

- Could only the portion of the 19 acre site west of the college access drive be purchased with a corresponding reduction in price? This would reduce the cost of the land but would still provide greater acreage than actually needed. It was also felt that by offering to let the college retain the entrance drive, it would be an added inducement for their trustees to approve the sale.

- Determine the real asking price inasmuch as the published price was completely unrealistic.

- Determine whether an arrangement might be worked out to relocate the college sign from the west side of the college entry drive to the east side of that drive.

AUGUST 1, 1989

Harry Hays reported that he was having difficulty getting answers from the Love company. They had been involved in a joint venture with Al Hoffman and Center Park Forty Associates who own the property to the west of the desired site where they have been attempting to develop an office park. Hays was able to report however that Hoffman looked favorably upon our potential acquisition of the college property. Hoffman felt that a church building would be a desirable neighbor and that our prospective purchase might help alleviate some of the pressure stemming from the ten- million dollar lawsuit which Hoffman had pending against the City of Town and Country. This lawsuit resulted from the city's refusal to grant Hoffman a building permit. Hoffmans group had previously been issued a permit by St. Louis County prior to Town and Country's annexation of this entire area.

AUGUST 8, 1989

Hays suggested that the property should sell at possibly $200,000 an acre and proposed that we frame an offer in the area of $150,000-$175,000 per acre. It was determined at this point that we should obtain a letter of appraisal on the property based on residential zoning.

AUGUST 23, 1989

Appraisal received from Edward Dinan, Vice President Colliers International Property Consultants, stating an appraised value of $3,255,000 for the 15 acres we desire or $217,000 per acre. Final negotiated cost came to $175,000 per acre.

SEPTEMBER 15, 1989

A sale contract was submitted offering to purchase the 15 acres at a price of $2,625,000. This became the basis for all subsequent negotiations.

NOVEMBER 8, 1989

A modified contract was submitted with a number of changes. The college had asked for a 200-foot wide no-build zone across the east end of the property. We offered a 50-foot no-build zone which was subsequently accepted. We also specified that the proposed building would be 60,000 sq. ft. with possible multiple structures. Response was received on December 6 signed by Richard C. Miller, Vice President of Love Properties, agreeing to most all proposed changes.

DECEMBER 7, 1989

A purchase contract was signed by Menlo F. Smith as purchaser and Love Corporate Partners as sellers. Purchase price $2,625,000 with a deposit of $50,000. Approval of the purchase contract by the Missouri Baptist College Board of Trustees was included with the contract.

MARCH 12, 1990

A geotechnical report was received from Shannon & Wilson Inc. of St. Louis rendering the opinion that the site is suitable for construction of the proposed building. An environmental assessment report was also received from Shannon & Wilson concluding that there were no hazardous wastes on the property.

MARCH 27, 1990

Letter received from Myron L. Sorensen, Counsel for the Church, authorizing Menlo F. Smith to accept the proposed contingencies in the purchase contract.

MAY 31, 1990

As purchaser, Menlo F. Smith, assigned all of his rights and interests in the property to the Church.

SEPTEMBER 6, 1990

The *St. Louis Post Dispatch* had somehow learned that we had acquired the college property and published a small two-column article announcing the purchase. Throughout the period of negotiation for the property and during the early planning stages, it was decided that every effort would be made to keep the purchase plans confidential and to avoid any publicity concerning plans for a temple in St. Louis. The *Post Dispatch* article stated in part:

> "The Church has no plans right now for the land but sees it as good for expansion," said Menlo F. Smith, the Regional Representative for the Quorum of the Twelve, the governing body of the Church of Jesus Christ of Latter-day Saints... "our Church is a growing Church and we maintain an inventory for future building sites," Smith said recently.

A major article appeared in the News Analysis section of the St. Louis Post Dispatch announcing a leadership change at Missouri Baptist College with Patrick O. Copley resigning as President and J. Edwin Hewlitt, Jr. - "taking over after a period marked by administrative problems and staff upheaval." Hewlitt was appointed on an interim basis to serve as President.

Other points mentioned in the *Post Dispatch* article included:

> "Recently, the college had reported operating with a balanced budget for the past four years. In large part, that was due to the sale of 35 acres, enabling the school to pay off about two-million dollars in accumulated debt."

The foregoing item has reference to the sale of land by the college to Love Properties including the 19 acre parcel from which the purchase by the Church came.

December 18, 1990

A letter was addressed to General Authorities and Regional Representatives and Stake Presidents in the midwestern United States announcing construction of a temple in the St. Louis, Missouri area. Excerpts from the letter included the following statements:

> "We are pleased to announce the selection of a site and an intent to construct a temple in the St. Louis Missouri area."

> "We are confident that this will be a blessing to the many faithful Saints in this and the surrounding areas who have had to travel long distances to enjoy the blessings of the temple."

December 18, 1990

To: General Authorities; and the following priesthood leaders in the Midwestern United States: Regional Representatives and Stake Presidents

Dear Brethren:

Construction of Temple in the St. Louis, Missouri Area

We are pleased to announce selection of a site and an intent to construct a temple in the St. Louis, Missouri area.

We are confident that this will be a blessing to the many faithful Saints in this and surrounding areas who have had to travel long distances to enjoy the blessings of the temple. Specific stakes to be included in the temple district will be announced at a later date.

Members who desire to contribute financially toward construction of the temple may be invited to do so as their circumstances permit. In harmony with the spirit of the local unit budget allowance program, local priesthood leaders should not conduct fund-raising efforts, or establish assessments or goals for this purpose.

Members making donations for temple construction can indicate "temple" on the "other" line of the donation receipt. Wards will transfer these funds by check to Church headquarters monthly. Priesthood leaders will not receive reports from Church headquarters summarizing these contributions.

We commend the Saints for their devotion and faithfulness, and are thankful for the blessings that will come to them through the erection of this new temple.

Faithfully your brethren,

The First Presidency

Official Letter of intent to build a temple in St. Louis, Missouri, from the First Presidency of the Church.

"We commend the Saints for their devotion and faithfulness, and are thankful for the blessings that will come through the erection of this temple."

DECEMBER 29, 1990

A second article appeared in the *Post Dispatch* regarding the temple following formal announcement by the First Presidency of plans to build a temple in the St. Louis area. This article made mention of Jim Robinson, who had recently been hired as City Administrator in Town and Country. It is interesting that Jim Robinson was hired just in advance of the time that the Church would be seeking approval from the city for construction of the new temple within the city boundaries. Brother Robinson grew up in St. Louis as a member of the Church, the son of George and Edith Robinson, long-time Church members in St. Louis.

MARCH-NOVEMBER 1991

Organization of a local Temple Task Force group was begun which included the following individuals:

- Richard Oscarson (real estate background)
- Kent Munson (attorney)
- John Lowe (architectural background)
- Keith Sawyer (regional public affairs director)
- Shirlene Bunnell (representing the Relief Society women)
- Cindy Pulley (media background)
- Bishop David Jensen (host ward for temple)

NOVEMBER 10, 1991

A preliminary meeting of the Temple Task Group was held. Menlo Smith offered in his comments as Chairman: "The Prophet Joseph Smith spoke of hundreds of temples. President Kimball spoke of thousands of temples dotting the earth. The St. Louis Temple is a part of those prophetic visions."

At this meeting, the group was informed that plans for the temple are to remain confidential and not to be discussed with anyone outside of the Task Group. Temples are the prerogative of the First Presidency. St. Louis is to set a new standard for temples. Our building is to be at least 40,000 sq. ft. with a single spire. It will not have a visitors center but will have an ancillary building of approximately 10,000 sq. ft. There will be possible provision for a future stake center on the site.

The role of the Temple Task Group would be to develop the strategy and prepare the presentation for obtaining approval from the city for construction of the temple and also to handle all public affairs and public information regarding the temple. It was established that we would not unveil our plans until the first public hearing and that the matter would be kept confidential in the meantime. It was learned at this meeting that there was to be an election in the City of Town and Country in April of 1992 where two of the present aldermen were to be up for re-election. It was concluded that every member of the committee would make every effort to identify everyone and anyone living within the City of Town and Country who might be helpful in the permitting process.

MARCH 17, 1992

A telephone call was received by Menlo Smith from Rodmar Pulley of the Temples and Special Projects Department informing that Hellmuth, Obata and Kassebaum had been selected as architects for the temple. Our own member, John Lowe, had been selected by HOK as client liaison.

In the meantime it was learned that Elizabeth "Betty" Perry, the Mayor of Town and Country had been a friend of the Menlo Smith's years ago when both families lived in Kirkwood and their children attended the Henry Hough School together. Betty Perry subsequently proved to be a great friend. She could not have been more supportive and helpful during the course of the permitting process had she been the Stake Relief Society President.

MARCH 31, 1992

A meeting of the Temple Task Group was held where tentative plans were set to make the permit application in June or July. A timeline was agreed upon as follows:

- November/December - submit plans for approvals.
- Bid opening July 1, 1993.
- Groundbreaking - September 1, 1993.
- Construction - two years.
- Dedication - fall 1995

JULY 1, 1992

Meeting of Temple Task Group. It was announced that Robert Dewey of the Church Architectural Department would be the Architect-of-Record for the temple. Rod Pulley agreed to open a channel of communication between the

Temple Task Group and the architectural department of the Church. The Temple Task Group requested the opportunity to assemble of list of suggestions pertaining to the functional aspects of the temple design. It was agreed that the Chairman, Menlo Smith, would compile and distill suggestions received and convey these to the Church architects through Rod Pulley. This was done and the entire committee was subsequently elated upon learning that virtually every suggestion offered was to be incorporated into the design of the temple.

Subsequent to the foregoing, the Temples and Special Projects Department of the Church determined that it was advisable to select an architect other than HOK of St. Louis. As a result, the firm of Chiodini and Associates of St. Louis was selected to handle the project. The firm proved to be excellent both from a technical standpoint as well as with respect to their judgement in proposing a very traditional design which proved to be appropriate for and warmly received by the St. Louis community. The firm was also very effective in working with the City of Town and Country throughout the permitting process.

AUGUST 3, 1992

Luncheon meeting with Dr. Thomas S. Field, Acting President of Missouri Baptist College. This meeting was arranged by Jay Carter, a friend of Menlo Smith. Mr. Carter has had a long-time relationship with Missouri Baptist College and at one time belonged to the Baptist Church. This meeting also included Richard Oscarson, St. Louis Stake President. The meeting was arranged for the purpose of getting acquainted and establishing a relationship with the college. It became quite clear in the discussion that Dr. Field strongly disagreed with the decision made by his predecessor to sell the campus property and felt that the property we purchased was the most valuable of any of the college property. In jest, Dr. Field suggested that we should build our temple to look like a college administration building and then let them leave their sign on the property where it is presently located. It was learned during the conversation that the college has reacquired the 14 acres in Creve Coeur which had been part of the original parcel owned by Love from which our ground was divided.

OCTOBER 18, 1992

In the Temple Task Group meeting Robert Dewey, Church Architect, advised that plans for the temple are moving forward. The building is to measure approximately 85' x 180' and will consist of three levels with four endowment rooms and the Celestial Room at the east end of the building on the upper floor with sealing rooms to the west. Groundbreaking is anticipated mid-1993 with an estimated two years for completion.

NOVEMBER 3, 1992

Rod Pulley advised that in response to the suggestion from our Temple Task Group an investigation had been conducted about the possible use of Nauvoo limestone for the temple. The stone from the Nauvoo Temple had come from three different quarries. Two of them are now flooded but samples were taken from a third. The whiteness was reported as excellent and that it compared favorably with the original. However it was finally concluded that the stone was too soft to be suitable for our St. Louis Temple.

We were also advised that it would be necessary to make application to the City of Town and Country to obtain special status as a "Recognized Church" in order that we can build on the property which is zoned for single family residences. Menlo Smith was asked to handle this part of the application process.

DECEMBER 14, 1992

The Board of Aldermen of the City of Town and Country approved by a vote of 7-0 issuance of a resolution classifying The Church of Jesus Christ of Latter-day Saints as a qualifying church and thus eligible to develop the property on North Outer Forty Drive.

As a result of the foregoing approval it now became possible to request a hearing by the City Planning and Zoning Commission in January at which time we would formally present our application for site plan approval. To assure success in that meeting, it was decided that the Temple Task Group should begin making informal briefing contacts with members of the Planning Commission and the Board of Aldermen. Also it was determined that we would identify every person we could, members and non-members alike, who would be willing to appear at the January meeting in order to give support to our presentation and hopefully to occupy every available seat in the hearing room.

DECEMBER 29, 1992

Special planning meeting of the Temple Task Group to review strategy for the January meeting before the City Planning and Zoning Commission.

During this period numerous contacts were made with Jim Robinson, City Administrator, as well as with Mayor Betty Perry. Both were very helpful in guiding us through the permitting process, although no special favors were requested nor received.

JANUARY 27, 1993

Meeting of the Planning and Zoning Commission of the City of Town and Country at the City Hall. This meeting was set for 7:30pm. Arrangements had been made previously to have all of those appearing in our behalf arrive at the City Hall hearing room at 7pm in order that we could occupy as many seats as possible. To our dismay, the room was already filled upon our arrival. While no opposition of any kind had been encountered up to now, it seemed evident that opposition was now out in force. To our surprise, however, those in the hearing room were there, not to oppose us, but to oppose a decision that had been made previously by the Board of Aldermen to approve a re-zoning which would enable the expansion and development of a large shopping center on a main thoroughfare in the south part of the city. Ours was the last item on the agenda and by the time our turn on the agenda came, these irate residents were so tired and disgusted that they left. As a result we had the balance of the meeting virtually to ourselves. No one present voiced any opposition and many in our group, members and non-members alike, voiced support such that the tenor of the meeting was very positive and favorable.

Introductory remarks offered by Menlo Smith at the meeting included the following:

- Introduction of himself as a lay leader of the Church having administrative responsibility relating to the temple and other Church matters.

- The Church consists of eight million members with headquarters in Salt Lake City. We are perhaps best known and recognized for the Mormon Tabernacle Choir. Mentioned early Church history in Missouri and the persecution that developed, emphasizing that St. Louis became a haven for those so persecuted. It is fitting now that one of our most sacred buildings should be located in St. Louis.

- Clarified purposes of the building including:
  - Not a church meetinghouse; closed on Sundays.
  - Used for marriages, baptisms and sacred instruction.
  - Building will house no large meetings, only individual and family groups.
  - One of forty such temples worldwide, including: Salt Lake City, Washington, DC, London, Tokyo, etc.
  - We desire to produce a beautiful landmark structure in which Town and Country can take great pride. Assured the Commission that they would feel that way about it when it is complete.

- Introduced Lou Chiodini and the other professionals participating in the project including Steve Hermann, Architect, Myron Grimme, Landscape Architect, Rhine Dabler, Clayton Engineering Representative and Carl Hawk, Ross and Barrzini, Engineers.

The proposal for our site plan was then presented by Lou Chiodini with comments from the various professionals present. Responses to questions were given and finally, supporters were invited to stand. Every person in the room stood up. No final action was taken at the meeting. We were informed that recommendations of the Commission would be presented at their February 24, 1993 meeting.

Subsequently plans were formulated for additional contacts with key people including Mayor Perry, Jim Robinson, Vaughn Morse and Joan Corderman, the latter two being Aldermen for the area in which the temple property is located. Plans were also made to contact nearby property owners. Contacts were made with bishops of wards throughout the stake asking them to encourage their members to include this matter in their prayers and to ask the Lord to soften the hearts of those in authority that they would respond favorably to the request for approval of this temple project. Contact was also made with a number of residents of Town and Country requesting that they write letters of support to the Mayor recommending approval of our project which many did.

FEBRUARY 24, 1993
Public hearing of the Planning and Zoning Commission. Again every effort was made to have supporters in attendance at this hearing, arriving at least 30 min-

utes early in order to fill the seats in the hearing room. As with the prior hearing, the room was already filled upon our arrival. Again, those present were residents who were upset about the approval of the shopping center development in another part of the city. They again occupied the greater part of the meeting with their deliberations and then left, tired and harried, having little concern for our proposed temple project. The balance of the meeting thus went smoothly with no opposition and resulted in favorable recommendation for our project by the Planning and Zoning Commission.

MARCH 15, 1993

Meeting of the Town and Country Board of Aldermen to consider final approval for our proposed site development plan. Once again, upon arrival of our group, the hearing room was already largely filled. And as had been the case previously, those present were focused entirely on the issue of the shopping center development and not the least interested in our plans to build a temple. So once again we were blessed and helped by circumstances over which we had no control and little influence but which culminated such that we had no opposition to our proposal. Virtually all present were there to support our plans.

Alderman Joan Corderman offered Bill #93-15, an Ordinance (#1663) proposing approval of our preliminary site development plan for the temple. After the presentation had been completed, one of the aldermen said, "This seems to be fine but you have not yet shown us what the building is going to look like architecturally." At this point Lou Chiodini removed a covering from the architectural rendering of the temple which was mounted on a tripod in the room but which up to this point was not visible. When the covering was removed, the entire room as one voice uttered an audible sigh of amazement at the beauty of this building which was now for the first time evident. For some several minutes, no one in the room spoke. Finally, Alderman Vaughn Morse stood and said, "I am not going to move approval of this project!" There was then a long pause during which our hearts sank. Alderman Morse then continued, "I move unanimous and enthusiastic approval of this project." An unanimous vote was then recorded following which the entire room broke into applause. The aldermen were happy with their decision and proud to have made it possible to bring this beautiful edifice to their city. All representing the Church were of course elated.

MARCH 22, 1993

Meeting of the Board of Adjustment of the City of Town and Country. Application was presented for a variance for the height of our building, for the height of the steeple and for the height of our fence. Chiodini had been requested to prepare large display boards showing contiguous elevations of the various buildings along North Outer Forty Drive from the Missouri Highway Department radio antenna just west of Mason Road eastward to include all of the office buildings and the high tension power lines to the west of our property as well as our proposed building with its steeple. When these boards were held up contiguously for the Board of Adjustment members, it was quickly evident that even though our building would exceed the allowable height, it would nevertheless be at a lower elevation than the other buildings along this corridor. When we also pointed out that the steeple on the Presbyterian Church known as Kirk of the Hills was three feet higher than our proposed steeple, any opposition that might have existed to our proposal for variance quickly melted. Request for variance from the regulation 4' high fence limit was made on the basis that this would be one of the most beautifully landscaped buildings in all of Town and Country and that a higher fence was needed to assure that vandals and others would not enter the property and cause damage. When they were shown that the fence would be a beautiful ornamental iron fence, approval on this as well as on the building and steeple height were given.

APRIL 6, 1993

A city election was held wherein a slate of candidates had been proposed by the dissidents opposing the shopping center development. They hoped to completely replace the Board of Aldermen, as well as the Mayor. Every effort had been made to assure that the final hearing would precede this election out of concern for the potential constituency of the Board of Aldermen and the apparent mentality of those who were running on this slate. As it turned out Mayor Betty Perry was defeated by seven votes and approximately half of the Board of Aldermen was replaced with dissidents. Had the final hearing occurred following this election it is likely that our proposal would have been defeated and perhaps delayed indefinitely.

In review it is abundantly evident that the hand of the Lord has been upon this project from the beginning as evidenced by the following:

- The property came on the market just shortly before the decision was made to acquire a site for a temple in St. Louis. Because of the desirability of the site, had it been available further in advance, its most likely that it would have been purchased by others.

* As a result of the shakeup in leadership at the Missouri Baptist College, had we not succeeded in concluding a contract for the purchase of the site when we did, it would likely have been impossible to do so several weeks later after the shakeup occurred. The position of the new president was that he would not have permitted sale of the property.

* But for the financial circumstances of the college, the property would not have been available. The developers of the property found themselves in difficult straits as a result of tightening credit in the real estate market and this prompted their need to offer the property for sale at exactly the right moment.

* The availability of Mayor Betty Perry and City Administrator Jim Robinson at a crucial time in the approval process proved to be immensely helpful. Betty Perry was defeated a few days following final approval. Jim Robinson has since moved on to pursue other opportunities.

All of the foregoing occurred with absolutely no public opposition, a situation almost unheard of in the history of the Church with regard to the construction of new temples. The hand of the Lord must be acknowledged in all this, without which the successful outcome could not have been realized.

AUGUST 31, 1993

Meeting of the St. Louis Temple Dedication Committee, held at the Temple Department at Church Headquarters in Salt Lake City. Present were Elder W. Eugene Hansen, Brothers Derek F. Metcalfe, John E. Hardy and Menlo F. Smith. Also present was the Area Presidency in the North America Central Area including James M. Paramore, William R. Bradford and Hartman Rector, Jr. Elder W. Eugene Hansen presided. Highlights of the meeting included:

* Date and time for the groundbreaking for the St. Louis Temple was established at 2pm October 30, 1993.

- Project construction manager was announced as Gary Holland.

- A coordinating meeting was set to be held in conjunction with October General Conference to which Menlo Smith would be invited to review plans and preparations for the groundbreaking ceremony.

SEPTEMBER 27, 1993

Ordinance #1712 was approved amending Ordinance #1663 revising the preliminary site development plan and allowing all requested changes and variances.

LAND HISTORY OF TEMPLE SITE

The previous ownership of the temple site belonged to the Sellenreik Family farm, including 120 acres. The father died leaving the property to his wife. As the three sons married, they received three acres on the north of 40 as a wedding gift. They each eventually sold their acreage. The fourth brother, Erwin, took care of his mother until her death and inherited the remaining land. Erwin worked the land until 1972. In 1973, Erwin sold the land to the Missouri Baptist College.

two • GROUNDBREAKING

The groundbreaking for the St. Louis Missouri Temple was held on October 30, 1993 at 2pm. The day included freezing temperatures and snow flurries, despite which attendance was estimated in excess of 5,000 persons. President Gordon B. Hinckley, First Counselor in the First Presidency of the Church, presided at the ceremony.

The temple site served as an ideal location for the Groundbreaking event. Just north and east of the crest of the hill where the temple would be situated, was a circular slope dropping into the wooded area to the north and east forming a natural amphitheater. A covered stand was constructed against the backdrop of the woods facing southwest. This made for a secluded setting shielded from the highway sounds by the natural terrain. The site was prepared by installation of a gravel road leading into the site. The level area on the west portion of the site provided substantial parking which was supplemented through the kindness of the owners of the nearby office buildings who made their parking lots available to handle the overflow.

Nestled between the banks of the mighty Missouri and Mississippi Rivers is a place where early pioneers stopped to outfit before adventuring into the wilderness. The place is called St. Louis. Known as the "Gateway to the West," St. Louis became a popular haven for weary travelers, an oasis along the trail where one could pause to reflect on the past, and to contemplate the challenges ahead. To some, St. Louis was the last refuge of hope, while for others, it was a new beginning for a brighter tomorrow. Established as a community before our young country was established as a nation, St. Louis was well advanced over the surrounding frontier in terms of providing such amenities as education, cultural attributes and churches. As pioneers gathered, they sought out other individuals with common interests. Many found a common bond through their faith in God. Thus St. Louis became a place of religious freedom.

It was during this time that one of the earliest stakes of The Church of Jesus Christ of Latter-day Saints was organized in St. Louis. Many of the Saints and early founders of the Church sought and received refuge in St. Louis after having been driven and persecuted elsewhere for their faith in God. It is fitting that, just as those early Saints were given haven in St. Louis, this same community has graciously welcomed the announcement of plans for the construction of a House of the Lord.

Today, ground is being dedicated and hallowed for this sacred edifice. Here, standing atop the peaceful promontory, will be a Temple of the Lord - a tribute to those who endured the hardships of the past and to the community which gave them refuge; a promise of life everlasting to those who enter its doors in the years to come.

GROUNDBREAKING SERVICE RECOGNITION

CITY OF TOWN AND COUNTRY
Mayor Peggy Symes
Aldermen and women: Tom Etling, Steve Hamilton,
Sandra Felkner, and Peter Martin
Members of Planning and Zoning Commission and other City Officials:
James Robinson, City Administrator
Nels Brown, Director of Development Committee
Sharon Rothmel, Planning Director
Skip Delmar, Police Chief and staff

CHIODINI AND ASSOCIATES – ARCHITECTS
Louis Chiodini and staff

MISSOURI BAPTIST COLLEGE
President Thomas Field
Dr. Arlen Dykstra, Dean

MEDICAL
St. John's Mercy Medical Center staff

MEDIA
St. Louis Post-Dispatch

STATE OF MISSOURI
John Ashcroft, previous Governor of Missouri
Janet Ashcroft

CHURCH
President and Sister Gordon B. Hinckley
President and Sister Thomas S. Monson
Elder Dallin H. Oaks
Elder James M. Paramore
Elder and Sister Hartman Rector, Jr.
Roy and Vera Oscarson, Coordinator of Groundbreaking Events
Menlo F. and Mary Jean Smith
Boyd and Verelee Schenk
Fred and Jean Farmer
Grant and Dorthy Rees
Mission President and Sister Wayne McGrath
Regional Representatives
Stake Presidents and wives, representing twenty-eight stakes
Patriarchs

SAINT LOUIS MISSOURI TEMPLE

GROUNDBREAKING SERVICE

– 30 October 1993 –

PRESIDING
Presidency

CONDUCTING
President Gordon B. Hinckley, First Counselor in the First Presidency

COMBINED REGIONAL CHOIR
"The Lord's Prayer"

MUSIC DIRECTOR
Sister Larrie Christensen

ORGANIST
Sister Heather James

INVOCATION
Elder James M. Paramore, Quorum of the Seventy

SPEAKERS
Dallin H. Oaks, Quorum of the Twelve Apostles
President Thomas S. Monson, Second Counselor in the First Presidency

COMBINED REGIONAL CHOIR
"Song of Praise"

REMARKS OF THE DEDICATION SITE
President Gordon B. Hinckley, First Counselor in the First Presidency

COMBINED REGIONAL CHOIR AND CONGREGATION
"I Know That My Redeemer Lives"

BENEDICTION
Elder Hartman Rector, Jr., Member of the Seventy

GROUNDBREAKING
President Gordon B. Hinckley, under the Direction of the First Presidency

President Gordon B. Hinckley and President Thomas S. Monson of the First Presidency and Elder Dallin H. Oaks of the Quorum of the Twelve Apostles greet members at the temple groundbreaking on the cold Missouri day. President Hinckley presided over the ground breaking ceremony for the St. Louis Missouri Temple.

GROUND BREAKING CEREMONY FOR THE ST. LOUIS, MISSOURI TEMPLE HELD SATURDAY, OCTOBER 30, 1993 AT 2:00 PM ON THE TEMPLE SITE IN THE CITY OF TOWN AND COUNTRY

President Gordon B. Hinckley, First Counselor in the First Presidency, conducting. (The temperature was 35 degrees with occasional snow flurries.)

PRESIDENT HINCKLEY: We are two or three minutes ahead of time but let's beat the blizzard. We welcome each of you this afternoon to the ground breaking service for the St. Louis Missouri Temple. We appreciate your devotion and sacrifice in making the effort to be with us. I think this is the first time I've ever conducted a meeting in an overcoat. I hope that all of you are warm and comfortable. If not, I have a hat I can spare right here.

We extend to you the love and greetings of President Ezra Taft Benson who due to reasons of health must be excused. We acknowledge President Thomas S. Monson second counselor in the First Presidency, Elder Dallin H. Oakes, member of the Quorum of the Twelve Apostles, Elders James M. Paramore, and Hartman Rector of the Seventy and their wives. Seated immediately in front of the stand are the regional representatives and stake presidents for the 27 stakes in the St. Louis Missouri Temple District, the president of the Missouri St. Louis Mission and the wives and families of these brethren. We're honored with the presence of Mayor Peggy Symes who presides as Mayor of the City of Town and Country in which this site is located; and also the following Aldermen and women who's presence we recognize and deeply appreciate; Tom Edtling, Steve Hamilton, Sandra Feltner, Peter Martin, members of the Planning and Zoning Commission and other city officials including James Robinson, City Administrator, Nels Brown, Director of the Development Committee, Sharon Rothmill, Planning Director, and Police Director Skip Delmar and his staff who have been very gracious in assisting on this occasion.

We recognize Mr. Louis Chiodini and staff of the firm of Chiodini and Associates who are working as architects on this temple. We're indebted to President Thomas Field of the Missouri Baptist College, who's asked to be excused because of his wife's illness. But we have Dr. Arlan Dykster, the Dean, and other staff members. We're grateful for the assistance of the St. John's Mercy Medical staff and the media who are represented here on this occasion.

We recognize Roy Oscarson, Coordinator Ground Breaking Activities; President and Sister Thomas H. Monson, Elder Dallin H. Oakes, Brother Paramore, Brother Rector and their wives, Mission President and Sister Wayne McGrath and other church officers who are here and are pleased to acknowledge the presence of the past Governor of Missouri, John Ashcroft and his wife, Janet. Thank you for being here.

We pay special tribute to Elder Paramore who serves as chairman of this occasion and also as President of the North America Central Area of the Church and are very deep and specially grateful to Brother Menlo F. Smith, who has been the real wheel-horse in arranging these many, many things and who has been assisted by many others to whom we express our deep gratitude.

The music this afternoon will be provided by a combined regional choir from the St. Louis area under the direction of Sister Larrie Christensen, with Sister Heather James providing the accompaniment. The choir will begin this service by singing "The Lord's Prayer". The invocation will then be offered by Elder James M. Paramore of the Seventy.

Choir -"The Lord's Prayer"

JAMES M. PARAMORE: Our beloved Father in Heaven. Our hearts are touched as we assemble this morning on this special place upon the earth. And we thank thee, Father in Heaven, for thy Beloved Son, Jesus Christ, and for His leadership of thy kingdom here upon this earth. We're thankful that He came to a young prophet, Joseph Smith, and re-established upon this earth, the eternal ordinances that will permit us to walk back into thy presence, clothed with glory and eternal lives. Dearly beloved Father, we recognize that this day is the commencement of a sacred building that in effect will be a bridge between earth and heaven wherein all of thy children, who so desire, may learn more of thee by entering therein and by receiving ordinances and covenants which will permit them to better understand thy holy ways and to find themselves sealed together in families into the eternities.

We recognize, Heavenly Father, that this will be the possibility for all of thy children who have ever come to earth, or who yet will come, to have these blessings in their lives, in their families, for all eternity. We love thee, Father in Heaven, and we pray that those who will speak this day, the Presidency of this

Church, one of thy Apostles, that they will have thy Spirit to be with them and that all who are here will remember this sacred occasion and even plan for the culmination of the work that begins today. We're grateful, Father in Heaven, for the truths that have been restored to this earth and for the power they are in our lives, to walk more fully in the ways of thy Beloved Son, Jesus Christ. Give us the power, the strength and the courage to follow Him that all that thou hast may be ours. We ask thy blessings to be upon those who are here and who will return to their homes, that they will be protected. We ask that those who will work in this sacred edifice will also be protected and nothing will hamper thy work or their work; and we thank thee again, Father in Heaven, for this special opportunity to be here as brothers and sisters in thy kingdom and we utter this prayer and these feelings of our heart, in the name of thy son, Jesus Christ, AMEN.

PRESIDENT HINCKLEY: We shall now be pleased to hear remarks from Elder Dallin H. Oakes of the Quorum of the Twelve Apostles. He asked me on the plane how long he should speak. I said about as long as the ice icicles on the noses of those on the back row. Elder Oakes.

DALLIN H. OAKES: My brothers and sisters, you're aware of the instructions that I have received and you can judge whether I am true to them. We are grateful for the wonderful music of the choir and for your presence here in such impressive numbers. This is such a marvelous occasion. We gather here because of the vision of the prophets of God that a house of the Lord should be built in this place and because of the generosity and faithfulness of tithe payers of the church, in all parts of the world, making possible the building, of what the scripture refers to, as the mountain of the Lord's house. This is a familiar scriptural reference to a Temple of the Lord. The mountain of the Lord's house suggests that we go to high ground.

When we come to a house built to the Lord we go to a high ground literally in this wonderful place. Mayor Symes, we're grateful to be here in Town and Country on this lovely site. We came to the mountain of the Lord's house to take higher ground in a figurative sense as well. When I was teaching at the University of Chicago many years ago, I had a colleague who wrote a book called *"What Knowledge Is Most Worth Having"*. Some knowledge is more important than others. The Lord's house gives us the knowledge that is of greatest worth in an eternal sense. It teaches us the nature of God. It teaches us the need for a Savior. It teaches us the purpose of our life and our destiny if we make and keep sacred covenants. The Lord's house provides us an opportunity to learn of our responsibilities to God and our responsibilities to one another. That is the reason why so many of us gather here in this beautiful place to commemorate the ground breaking for a House of the Lord and I say that in seriousness; and then in semi-seriousness may I say that those of us who come from outside the State of Missouri, are certainly grateful for the warm Missouri welcome that you have given us on this occasion. The weather is threatening but the occasion is an occasion for celebration. Our hearts are warm and our feelings of love for one another and gratitude for our Heavenly Father are supreme on this occasion. May God bless us in this enterprise I pray as I testify to you of Jesus Christ who's house this is, in the name of Jesus Christ AMEN.

PRESIDENT HINCKLEY: Thank you, Elder Oakes. President Thomas S. Monson second counselor in the First Presidency will now speak to us and the choir will then sing "Song of Praise". President Monson.

PRESIDENT THOMAS S. MONSON: I had about the same experience as Brother Oakes. I said to Sister Monson, "what should I speak about this morning?" She said, "About 5 minutes." She's a very quiet girl except when she wants to give me a word or two.

As I saw Menlo Smith this morning I thought, many's the time in the Philippines with the hot, humid weather, he and Sister Smith would long for a day like this. And of course, my mind went back to the time that I had the opportunity and the assignment to turn the sod for the temple in Stockholm, Sweden. I think it was early April. It was cold, real cold and they had to use a blow torch to loosen a little soil so that we could turn the sod. What a happy day.

As I see you assembled on this knoll, I cannot help but think of the words of holy scripture where one day during the personal ministry of our Lord, he took Peter and James and John with him up unto an high mountain and was transfigured before them; and his face did shine as the light, the sun, and his raiment was white as the light. And behold, there appeared unto them Moses and Elias, talking with him. Then answered Peter, and said unto Jesus, "Lord, it is good for us to be here." And I simply say unto our Heavenly Father, in behalf of all assembled and to his Son, Lord, it's good for us to be here.

This is an historic place in church history through the years, not just recently, but in years long ago. I jotted down a note from the *St. Louis Luminary*, a church newspaper, written February 3, 1855, and I quote: "This city has been an asylum for our people from 15 to 20 years. There's probably no city in the world where the Latter-day Saints are more respected and where they may sooner obtain an outfit for Utah. The hand of the Lord is in these things." I recall too, that in this area the first stake of the church was organized, a long time ago. Remember too, that the papyri and the mummies that Joseph Smith has become famous for, were displayed here in this city. And being a printer and publisher formerly, I like to recall that the casting for the font of type for the alphabet took place here in St. Louis. And I still have a few copies of that Deseret alphabet and I'm so grateful that Brigham Young ceased the idea of introducing a new language with a new alphabet. I'm very happy with what we have.

I think it's significant that on June 1, 1958 a hundred years after the original stake was dissolved because the emigrants went to the West, the St. Louis Stake was again organized with Elders Harold B. Lee and Mark E. Peterson presiding. These are very influential men and I think with their pervasive capacities our Heavenly Father would permit them to look in on what they did here way back in 1958.

In reading the history of St. Louis and the environs round about I touched a familiar and a heartfelt note when I recognized that 1849 was a very difficult year for the Latter-day Saints who came to St. Louis. My mother's forebears were in the company from Scotland that came all the way from New Orleans to St. Louis to earn a little money that they might equip and go west, to the city and the heights of the mountains, but they ran into a very difficult problem here. One word, cholera. Ever so many of the Saints suffered from that dread disease. From the journals of my forebears I read, "They arrived in St. Louis in 1849 en route to Salt Lake City. Son, William, age 18, died there June 22, 1849. Mother, Mary, died there June 27, five days later. Son, Archibald, age 15, died two days later. And husband, Charles, died July 4, a week later." Four from one family, leaving my great, great grandmother an orphan with her brothers and sisters to hitch a ride and make their way westward.

I think of the words of the great pioneer hymn, "And should we die before our journey's through, All is well, all is well. We then are free from care and sorrow too, All is well". I feel I'm standing on sacred ground in an area where my dear forebears completed their trek to find God and to establish his kingdom here upon the earth.

Now there are happier days than those when I reflect upon St. Louis. I remember when I called Roy Oscarson. I had an assignment to come here and this pleasant soul said to me, "Brother Monson, do you like baseball?" I said, "I happen to love baseball." There was a long pause. He said, "Thank heaven, thank heaven." He said, "I've got tickets to the world series. Would you like to go." I said, "By all means!" "Could we alter the meeting schedule on Saturday?" I said, "By all means."

And didn't you know we had to pray just as hard that day as we prayed today because it was overcast; rain was pouring down, but by heavens, by noon, the rain had gone, the sun was shining, St. Louis beat Boston, and we had a wonderful time together. And, of course, when you think of Roy and his family, you can't help but think of the other great names in this area with whom I'm acquainted. I'll just jot a couple of them. I've taken them from my journal.

Take for example what I've written in my journal, June 19, 1971 - "At 7:30 this morning I met along with Elder Wirthlin, President and Sister Richard Oscarson, prior to their departure for the Sweden, Stockholm Mission. In my judgement Brother Oscarson is very much like his father, Roy, in leadership ability and devotion to the Swedish people. He's outstanding in every respect, as is his charming wife. They'll make a great contribution in Sweden."

October 4, 1979 - a number of years later. "In the afternoon I had the opportunity to hear the presidency report of President Paul Oscarson, who presided in the Sweden, Goteborg Mission. He was accompanied by his lovely wife, Bonnie. It was a delight to hear this outstanding young man make his report. He's endowed with administrative ability and a sweet sense of humility."

I continued, Don Oscarson, is also outstanding. You know they should have produced eight or ten children. He is the producer and director of the City of Joseph, the Nauvoo Pageant. Then I say a word about Bonnie and her comments about her family, the Oscarsons, in those days when this was an outpost for young people who were coming eastward to seek their fortune, but they hadn't had any fortune at that point, and they would stay with the Oscarsons and with the other families in this area. And we all know that Roy presided in Glasgow, the area where my mother's family came from. All three out presiding over missions at the same time.

And then what a delight to put an arm around the shoulder of my dear friend, Boyd Schenk today. My that brings back a lot of memories. And Henry Beal, and Mardean Steinmetz, and Patricia Keyes. And then I happen to see our dear president who I had not seen for a long while, namely as I reflect upon my records, Richard Grant Rees. I stayed in his home and I wrote this. "Roy Oscarson gave me a copy of the Oscarson Family history book. After saying my prayers Saturday evening at the home of our stake president, President Richard Grant Rees, I remained on my knees and began to thumb through the Oscarson book. I found it so fascinating that the time slipped by and to my amazement as I concluded that portion pertaining to Roy's family and Harry Oscarson who lived in our old ward, I discovered I had been on my knees for an hour and a half. As I read some of the beautiful comments in the book, however, I felt that was an appropriate posture while reading such sacred writings." Just a few memories from the past and from a small journal which I keep.

I love this comment from the church news. Roy again is speaking. This is in 1990. Quote, "I would say that the awareness of the Latter-day Saints and the respect for the people of the Church has changed from night to day since we've been here. The ongoing, continuing growth here has been very satisfying. Now we have a beautiful LDS community and other than a temple we have every program of the church." I say today, Roy, you now will have your temple as will all of the Saints of this temple district. I talked to some this morning who have come all the way from Kansas City, others from Leavenworth, and I know you've assembled from far and wide for this historic occasion. We build temples so that we might redeem our dead and so that we'll have an opportunity to perform those ordinances which we will take with us through eternity. When we build a temple we literally build ourselves. I like to think of the statement from the Doctrine and Covenants, the revelation given at the time of the Kirtland Temple. "Organize yourselves and prepare every needful thing and establish a house, even a house of prayer, a house of fasting, a house of faith, a house of learning, a house of glory, a house of order, a house of God." That will be our privilege. And as we build this temple I believe we build ourselves, for as the Apostle Paul declared, "Know ye not that ye are the temple of God and that the spirit of God dwelleth in you". I feel we become spiritually closer to God whenever we build such an edifice.

Francis and I were born in the year 1927. Interestingly, she was born on East 5th South in Salt Lake and I was born on West 5th South. Went to rival schools, she to East and I went to West. I also recall that our grandparents knew each other in Sweden way back in 1897 so she is happy to be here with me as well.

And as we were chatting on the way over here, she said, "That's a beautiful sight that's been selected." We recalled that every member of the First Presidency, President Benson, President Hinckley, Brother Monson, we had the opportunity individually to look at sites in St. Louis. I think Menlo Smith helped us look around. When we saw this one, each one of us individually, on different occasions, said "this is the site where a temple of God should be built." And here that opportunity will now come to fulfillment.

As you think of the year we were born, however, 1927, that's rich in history in St. Louis. The time of the great flight of Charles Lindbergh, and whenever I see his plane in a museum or statements in the airport pertaining to that plane, I love the name, the Spirit of St. Louis. It's a pioneering spirit and those of you who have helped established the Church in this area and continue to help it to grow are real pioneers.

Webster defines a pioneer as one who goes before showing others the way to follow. That is your privilege. That's our obligation and our opportunity. And I simply say, thanks be to God for a temple, a temple of the Lord to be erected here. That will be the true spirit of St. Louis. God bless you and thanks to you, all the dignitaries who are here today. Our Mayor, and aldermen and alderwomen, we're grateful to you who have come out on this brisk morning to join with us in preparation; and then this afternoon in the fulfillment of this historic event. May our Heavenly Father bless us, and all who labor in his cause and all who seek to do that which is right, I ask in the name of Jesus Christ, AMEN.

Choir - "Song of Praise"

PRESIDENT HINCKLEY: Thank you for that warm song. Following my remarks and dedication of this site, the choir and congregation will sing "I Know That My Redeemer Lives". The words of which are on the back of your printed program. Elder Hartman Rector, Jr. of the Seventy will then offer the benediction.

After the benediction we ask that you remain in your places for a few moments for the ceremonial breaking of the ground. We extend our gratitude and sincere appreciation for your attendance, for the beautiful music, for the law enforcement officers and city officials, and for all who have given of their time to assist in this service.

I think we'd better not be too long. We'd better break the ground before it freezes. I don't know where that's going to take place. I've been looking around for a soft spot. Where will the shovels go in? Right over there! Has it been pre-dug? What a wonderful occasion this is. This may sound strange but I'm rather glad its cold. I think it brings us to a greater appreciation for our forebears who left the State of Missouri in 1838 under the orders of the then, governor, in a great and tragic episode in the history of our people, and I think in the history of this great state. They left Far West where they had laid the cornerstones for a temple. Made the long march all the way across the state to the Mississippi, in some instances leaving a trail of blood in the snow, and found refuge in Quincy, Illinois from which place they later moved on to Nauvoo to build what then became the largest city in the State of Illinois and which they abandoned in 1846 to go West to establish themselves in the valleys of the Rocky Mountains from which place they have grown to be a mighty people.

How remarkable a thing it is that a comparative handful of stragglers who constituted The Church of Jesus Christ of Latter-day Saints have now grown to a membership of eight and one-half million people in 138 countries across the world. Magnificent and tremendous and miraculous has been the growth of this church where ever it has gone. As has been indicated, the City of St. Louis was an exception to what was found in other areas of Missouri, and particularly in Western Missouri. Here our people found welcome and comfort and some relief from the difficulties they had known. The *St. Louis Post Dispatch* carried a story a few years ago commenting on that and said that this was a city on the frontier large enough to accommodate our people when they came here and to provide for them a measure of relief and refuge and employment. I quote: "St. Louis was the only town in the middle-west large enough to give the Saints some degree of anonymity; cosmopolitan enough to be tolerant of a new and strange religion; and prosperous enough to provide work for new comers."

Orson Hyde came here in 1845 and made this report. "I was highly pleased with the spirit that prevails among the Saints in St. Louis. They're united in fellowship, they are one in heart, one in faith, and one in their resolutions to serve and honor the Lord, to uphold the regular authorities of the Church, to listen to the counsel and instruction of the twelve. The vigilant excursions of Brother Riley, the presiding elder together with all the official members of the Church are truly praiseworthy. They're infatigable in their labors to gather together all the scattered sheep and bring them back to the fold. They visit the sick and administer to their wants. They also remember the building of the temple. There is much interest felt by many in St. Louis for our cause. More or less are being baptized weekly and the Saints number between three and four hundred."

I guess that's about the number who are here today, who were there then. You have got to make better progress than that, brothers and sisters. President Monson has commented on this place as a stopping place as our people came from the British Isles and Europe. This was a scene of terrible tragedy. Hundreds and hundreds of them died here. A man could come down with cholera in the morning and be dead by nightfall. And it was not unusual nor uncommon, and from here up the Missouri to Winter Quarters near the present site of Omaha, there were frequent stops of the river boats to bury the dead along the banks of the river. Many of you visited the monument at Winter Quarters where are remembered some 600 of the 6000 who died between the Mississippi river and the Valley of the Great Salt Lake as our people made their way west, company after company, through the years until the building of the railroad in 1869.

I am grateful that we're here this day. As President Monson indicated, we came here, I came here, he came here, and then President Benson came here. We were taken around and shown six possible sites. And each one of us in turn said, "this is the place to build the temple." And we're so very grateful to the officials of this city of Town and Country who have cooperated generously and in a gracious and most helpful way in authorizing the permits which are necessary for the construction of the sacred house of the Lord.

Following this ground breaking today site work will go forward for a season but it will probably be Spring before the actual construction begins. It will take about two years, probably, to build the temple. That's what the architects say. It's my experience, it always takes longer than the architects say and costs more. But at that time we shall have a magnificent building here which will be seen by the millions who traverse up and down this freeway, and it will be looked upon as a place of holiness to the Lord; and for us in the Church, a place with special meaning. It will become the 50th operating temple in the Church. We now have 45 operating temples. I should say for those who are not of our faith who are here, that a temple serves a different purpose than our regular meeting houses of which we now have more than 10,000 across the earth. We have 45 operating temples. We have five, including this one under construction, and we have eight more on which we are working in various parts of the world.

Tomorrow I'm going to Hartford, Conn. to look at a site there. I've just been down in Brazil, and I've been in Africa recently looking for sites there; and I'd better not say anything else or you will know where these are going to be. There will be a story too, early in *Church News*.

Well thank you so very much. I'm satisfied that the Prophet Joseph smiles on us today and I'm satisfied that those who were with him in that long trek across Missouri, in the winter of 1838, smile upon us as they see what we begin here this day. Thank you for being here. May the Lord bless you. I invite each of you to join in a prayer of dedication of this site.

Oh God, our Eternal Father, we bow before thee in gratitude. We thank thee for this day when we begin the construction of what will become the fiftieth operating temple of The Church of Jesus Christ of Latter-day Saints which, when completed, will be dedicated to Thee and thy beloved Son as the House of the Lord.

We thank Thee for this choice ground on which it will stand. We thank Thee, for all who have been instrumental in acquiring it. We thank Thee for the skills and dedication of those who already have spent much time on architectural work and design. We thank Thee for the cooperation of the officials of this city in which this temple will stand and for all who have assisted to this date.

We thank Thee, above all, for the reason of its construction, that blessings made possible through the atonement of thy beloved Son, The Lord Jesus Christ, may come to the living and the countless legions of the dead whose eternal opportunities will be greatly enhanced by reason of the work which will be done in this sacred edifice. Now, dear Father, we dedicate and consecrate and set apart this ground as the site for the St. Louis Missouri Temple of The Church of Jesus Christ of Latter-day Saints.

We pray that thou wilt bless it and hallow it and sanctify it for the purpose for which it is now set apart. We pray that construction, once begun, may go forward without delay or interruption. We ask for thy watchful care for those who will labor here that they may be protected from accident and injury. We pray that each may be touched by thy holy spirit and realize that this house on which he or she labors is a unique and special building, a house of God which will be dedicated to thine eternal purposes for the blessing of thy sons and daughters of all generations.

We pray that there will not be irreverence or disrespect or vandalism of any kind or any behavior that will be out of harmony with the purpose for which this building will be constructed. We thank thee for thy faithful people, those across the world whose consecrated tithes make possible this sacred structure. We thank thee for thy people who serve with faith in thy holy houses where ever they may stand. We pray that this may become a scene of beauty to all who will look upon it now and through generations to come.

We thank thee for those who have labored long and hard in making the many arrangements for this day of ground breaking. May they be blessed for their service and find satisfaction in their hearts for the contribution they make to this, thy holy work. Now our beloved Father, as we break ground this day to initiate construction we feel to rededicate our lives and our talents to thy sacred work and to the blessing of all whose lives we could touch for good. To this end we seek thy blessing and give unto thee and unto our saviour, Thy Son, the honor and the praise and the glory in his holy name, even the name of Jesus Christ, AMEN.

Choir & Congregation - "I Know That My Redeemer Lives"

ELDER HARTMAN RECTOR JR: Our gracious and kind Heavenly Father, we are thankful unto thee Father, that once again a plot of ground has been dedicated in the sacred and consecrated lands of Missouri wherein a temple can be built and will be built. That families may be joined together with bonds stronger than death or resurrection and that they will go on living in obedience to thy commandments. But equally as important, that those who have died without making such eternal covenants with thee may have the privilege of having these covenants made in their behalf. Where they can accept and live according to thee in the spirit but be judged according to men in the flesh. Father we love thee, we reverence thee, we express our thanks and appreciation for thy tender mercies unto us, thy great goodness to thy children who love thee and keep thy commandments. We ask forgiveness for sins, look unto thee for our strength and we pray that this house may go forth from this time, that nothing will stop its building progress, and that its dedication will be the means of bringing many souls unto thee both living and dead; that all things might work together for the good of thy children, for we do it in the name of the Lord Jesus Christ, our Savior and Redeemer, AMEN.

PRESIDENT HINCKLEY: Now, we'll see what we can do with this Missouri clay.

For release on Sunday, October 30, 1993. From The Church of Jesus Christ of Latter-day Saints.

WEEK ENDING NOVEMBER 6, 1993

Church News THE CHURCH OF JESUS CHRIST OF LATTER-DAY SAINTS

Published by the Deseret News, Salt Lake City, Utah

GROUND BROKEN FOR SAINT LOUIS MISSOURI TEMPLE

St. Louis, Missouri – Ground breaking services were held today for the St. Louis Temple of The Church of Jesus Christ of Latter-day Saints.

President Gordon B. Hinckley and President Thomas S. Monson of the First Presidency presided at the services. Other General Authorities of the Church participating were Elder Dallin H. Oaks, of the Quorum of the Twelve Apostles and Elders James M. Paramore and Hartman Rector Jr. of the Presidency of the North America Central Area of the Church.

The temple will be built in the city of Town and Country, Missouri, on a 14-acre site, on the north side of Highway 40/I-64, approximately one-third mile west of

I-270. The property, adjoining the Missouri Baptist College, is on a prominent hill that will give passers-by a panoramic view of the structure.

The temple will be the first in Missouri. There are currently 45 operating temples worldwide. Others are under construction in Orlando, Florida and Bountiful, Utah. Ground was broken October 9, 1993 for the Mt. Timpanogos Temple in American Fork, Utah. Plans have also been announced for temples in Guayaquil, Equador; Bogota, Columbia; Preston, England; Hartford, Connecticut; Madrid, Spain and Hong Kong.

Site preparation will begin soon after the groundbreaking. A construction contract will be awarded, and it is anticipated that the temple will be ready for dedication in approximately two years. The exterior of the temple will be of white granite, and the spire will rise to 150 feet, topped by a gold-leafed statue of the Angel Moroni.

The three-floor building will have approximately 56,400 square feet of floor space, which will include four ordinance rooms, four sealing rooms, a Celestial Room, and a baptistry, as well as offices, a cafeteria, and service/maintenance facilities.

The landscaping of lawn, trees, shrubs, flowers, and walkways will be designed to blend into the natural wooded areas on the north and northwest portions of the property. The site will be enclosed by a decorative wrought iron fence. The St. Louis Missouri Temple will serve members of the Church residing in Missouri, Illinois, and portions of surrounding states.

Ground is broken on cold day for temple in St. Louis, Mo.

BY JOHN L. HART
Church News staff writer

ST. LOUIS, MO

On an icy day with cold reminiscent of that experienced by early Saints driven from their homes in this state a century and a half ago, ground was broken for what will be the Church's first temple in Missouri.

"This may sound strange, but I am rather glad it is cold," said President Gordon B. Hinckley. "I think it brings us to a greater appreciation for the Saints who left the state of Missouri in 1838 under the orders of the then governor, a tragic episode in the history of our people, and I think that it must be so for Missouri."

President Hinckley, first counselor in the First Presidency, and President Thomas S. Monson, second counselor in the First Presidency, took part Oct. 30 in the ceremonial start of construction for the St. Louis Missouri Temple, which will be the Church's 50th temple.

In contrast with the treatment early Saints received in this state, Church leaders of today were enthusiastically welcomed by the mayor, aldermen and alderwoman of the city of Town and Country, where the temple will be located, and by John Ashcroft, former Missouri governor, and other local officials. Town and Country is a suburb of St. Louis, about 10 miles west of the city center.

The temple will be built near Interstate 64, a major east-west freeway, and close to the interchange of this freeway with I-270, the area's principal belt route. Two previous temples were proposed in Missouri in the 1830s, at Independence and Far West, but plans were abandoned after mobs expelled the Saints.

The enthusiastic acclaim for the groundbreaking of the St. Louis temple was a typical response of an area that in times past offered refuge to Saints persecuted in the western parts of the state and in Illinois. St. Louis was also a major immigration center for European converts from 1840 to 1857. Many pioneers were outfitted in St. Louis for the trek west.

Despite temperatures that hovered near freezing, sharpened by an icy breeze, members began flocking to the site two hours early. After arrival, they clustered together in the fellowship of mutual shelter. A slope overlooking the speaker's platform formed a natural amphitheater — and windbreak — as snowflakes occasionally swirled from threatening skies. Nearly 5,000 people gathered and excitedly welcomed the General Authorities.

After the ceremony was concluded, hundreds of families were undeterred by the chill as they stayed around to turn over the loosened clay soil with gold-painted shovels and to shake hands with the General Authorities.

Church leaders in attendance included President Hinckley and his wife, Marjorie; President Monson and his wife, Frances; and Elder Dallin H. Oaks of the Council of the Twelve and his wife, June. Also in attendance

Continued on page 4

Right, President Thomas S. Monson assists a young girl, who takes a turn in breaking ground for the St. Louis Missouri Temple. Below right, choir provides music at groundbreaking. Below left, despite cold weather, nearly 5,000 people attend groundbreaking ceremony.

Photos by John L. Hart

Ground is broken for temple in St. Louis

Continued from page 3

were Elder James M. Paramore of the Seventy and president of the North America Central Area, who is chairman of the St. Louis Missouri Temple committee, and his wife, Helen; and Elder Hartman Rector Jr. of the Seventy, and first counselor in the area presidency, and his wife, Connie.

President Hinckley, President Monson and Elder Oaks spoke at the gathering. Elder Paramore offered the invocation and Elder Rector gave the benediction.

Regional representatives, including Menlo Smith who is vice chairman of the temple committee, and stake presidents of the 28 stakes in the seven-state temple district and their wives and families were also in attendance. Music was provided by a combined regional choir under the direction of Sister Larrie Christensen and accompanied by Heather James.

Members living in Missouri, Indiana, Kansas, Illinois, Kentucky, Nebraska and Tennessee are included in the temple district.

In his address, President Hinckley quipped, "We'd better hurry to beat the blizzard" and "We'd better break the ground before it freezes."

He observed that the Saints in 1838 had laid the cornerstone for a temple in Far West, just before the Missouri governor's extermination order that led to their flight as refugees "all the way across the state to the Mississippi River. They came leaving a trail of blood in the snow. They found refuge in Quincy, Ill., and the place where they later would found Nauvoo.

"They built what then became the largest city in the state of Illinois, which they abandoned in 1846 to go west to establish themselves in the valleys of the Rocky Mountains, where they have grown to become a mighty people. How remarkable a thing it is that a comparative handful of stragglers who constituted The Church of Jesus Christ of Latter-day Saints have now grown to a membership of 8.5 million people in 138 countries across the world. Magnificent and tremendous and miraculous has been the growth of the Church wherever it is found."

While these early Saints were persecuted and expelled from other areas in Missouri, particularly western Missouri, they were welcomed in St. Louis, he related.

"Here our people found a welcome and some relief from the difficulties they had known. The St. Louis Post Dispatch carried a story about the Church a few years ago commenting that:

"St. Louis was the only town in the middle west large enough to give the Saints some degree of anonymity, cosmopolitan enough to be tolerant of a new and strange religion, and prosperous enough to provide work for newcomers."

President Hinckley said that, in the years after the exodus from Nauvoo, illness ravaged many of the immigrating European converts who debarked at St. Louis. "It was a scene of terrible tragedy. Hundreds and hundreds of them died weekly. A man could come down with cholera in the morning and be dead by nightfall, which was not unusual nor uncommon. And from here up the Missouri River to Winter Quarters near the present site of Omaha, Neb., there were frequent stops of the riverboats to bury the dead along the banks of the river."

The site chosen for the St. Louis temple was approved individually by each member of the First Presidency, said President Hinckley. "We were taken around [individually] and shown six possible sites, and each one of us in turn said this is the place to build the temple."

He said that after the groundbreaking, site work would proceed immediately, but foundation work would probably be postponed until better weather in the spring. Construction of the temple would likely take about two years from then.

"At that time we shall have a magnificent building here that will be seen by millions who travel up and down this freeway. And it will be looked upon as a place of holiness to the Lord."

In conclusion, he remarked: "I am satisfied that the Prophet Joseph smiles on us today. And I am satisfied that those who were with him on that long trek across Missouri in the winter of 1838 smile upon us as they see what we begin here today."

President Monson, in his address, noted that the day of groundbreaking was a historic day in an area rich in Church history. He said that in his reading of the history of St. Louis and nearby environs, "I touched a familiar and a heartfelt note when I recognized that 1849 was a very difficult year for the Latter-day Saints who came to St. Louis." Among those who came that year were "my mother's forebears in a company from Scotland.

"But they ran into a very difficult problem here. One word — cholera. Ever so many of the Saints suffered from that dread disease. They arrived in St. Louis in 1849 en route to Salt Lake City. From the journals of my forebears I read:

" 'Son William, age 18, died here June 22, 1849. Mother, Mary [McGowan Miller] died here June 27, five days later. Son Archibald, age 15, died two days later, and husband, Charles [Stewart Miller] died July 4, a week later.' Four in one family! My great-grandmother was left an orphan with her brothers and sisters to make their way westward.

"I think of the words of the great pioneer hymn: 'And should we die before our journey's through . . . all is well! We then are free from toil and sorrow, too; . . . All is well! All is well!' ('Come, Come, Ye Saints,' Hymns, No. 30.)

"I feel I am standing on sacred ground in an area where these dear forebears of mine completed their trek to find God and to establish His kingdom here upon the earth."

President Monson recalled experiences from the pages of his own journal on a happier note in more recent times, and paid tribute to the modern pioneers in the area, including the family of Roy W. Oscarson, president of the St. Louis Stake when it was organized in 1958.

President Monson quoted Brother Oscarson's comment made in 1990: "I would say that the awareness of the Latter-day Saints and respect of people for the Church has changed from night to day since we've been here. The ongoing, continuing growth here has been very satisfying. Now we have a beautiful LDS community, and other than a temple, we have every program of the Church."

Responding to that comment, President Monson said, "Today, Roy, you have a temple, as will all of the Saints in this temple district."

Temples are built, he said, "so that we might redeem our dead and so we'll have an opportunity to perform those ordinances which we'll take with us through eternity. When we build a temple, we literally build ourselves. I believe we become spiritually closer to God whenever we build such an edifice."

He noted that Charles A. Lindbergh flew the aircraft, "The Spirit of St. Louis," in 1927, the year of President Monson's birth.

"I love the same — The Spirit of St. Louis.' It reflects a pioneer spirit. Those who helped establish the Church in this area and continue to help it grow are real pioneers.

"I simply say, 'Thanks be to God for a temple, a temple of the Lord, to be erected here. That will be the true spirit of St. Louis.' "

In his address, Elder Oaks said, "We gather here because of the vision of the prophets of God that a house of the Lord should be built in this place.

"And because the generosity and faithfulness of the tithe payers of the Church in all parts of the world makes possible the building of what the scriptures refer to as the Mountain of the Lord's house.

"This is a familiar scriptural reference to a temple of the Lord," he asserted. "The mount of the Lord's house suggests that we come to high ground when we come to a house built to the Lord. We come to high ground literally in this wonderful place.

"The Lord's house provides us an opportunity to learn of our responsibility to God and our responsibility to one another. That is the reason why so many of us gather here on this beautiful place to commemorate the groundbreaking for a house of the Lord.

He expressed appreciation for "the warm Missouri welcome" from local leaders. "The weather is threatening, but the occasion is an occasion for celebration; our hearts are warm and our feelings of love for one another and gratitude for our Heavenly Father are supreme on this occasion."

SECTION TWO

one • TEMPLE DESIGN AND CONSTRUCTION

he 14-acre temple site is in the city of Town and Country, Missouri on a prominent hill that gives passers-by a breathtaking panoramic view. The exterior of the temple is of white granite, with a majestic 150 foot-high spire, topped with a gold-leafed statue of Angel Moroni. The three-floor structure has approximately 56,400 square feet of floor space, and includes four ordinance rooms, four sealing rooms, a Celestial Room, and a baptistry, as well as a cafeteria and offices. The temple is enclosed by a decorative wrought-iron fence, while the landscaping of trees, shrubs, flowers and walkways have been designed to blend into the natural wooded areas on the north and northwest portions of the property.

In late 1992, the design contract for the temple was awarded to Chiodini Associates, an architectural firm in Clayton, Missouri. A group of about 6-8 designers, headed by architect, Steve Herman, of Chiodini Associates worked closely with Bob Dewey, a Church architect in Salt Lake City, who guided the progress with initial concepts and Church-approved floor plans. Initially, the Church issued a basic temple design, which Chiodini Associates then worked with to develop a structure they felt was not only appropriate for the area, but one that would also be approved by the Church and City of Town and Country.

Chiodini Associates looked at and visited about a dozen other Church temples, but felt very strongly that the St. Louis Temple should have a unique look and feel. However, they did take some influence from the Salt Lake Temple in a few elements, such as the tall, narrow arched windows topped with round windows, the vertical pilasters, and a cornice at the top of the structure.

Architectural rendering of St. Louis Missouri Temple by Chiodini Associates.

After various exterior studies and three to four months of floor plan re-designs, Chiodini Associates developed a very elegant, transitional design for the temple with very traditional elements. They wanted a building that symbolized a wholeness and solidarity of the Mormon religion; one that was recognizable, dignified, and had a strong sense of unity.

After a number of exterior design studies during a period of about six months, the group finalized their designs, which they then sent to Salt Lake City for approvals, during which the entire process went very smoothly. Once the plans were approved by both the City of Town and Country, and the Temples and Special Projects in Salt Lake City, Chiodini Associates began work with their engineers, and others to complete the project. This entire design process took about a total of one year, from beginning to end.

Chiodini Associates then worked closely with the Temples and Special Project Committee on the interior design of the temple, as well as with Myron Grimme on the landscaping, completing the project in April, 1997.

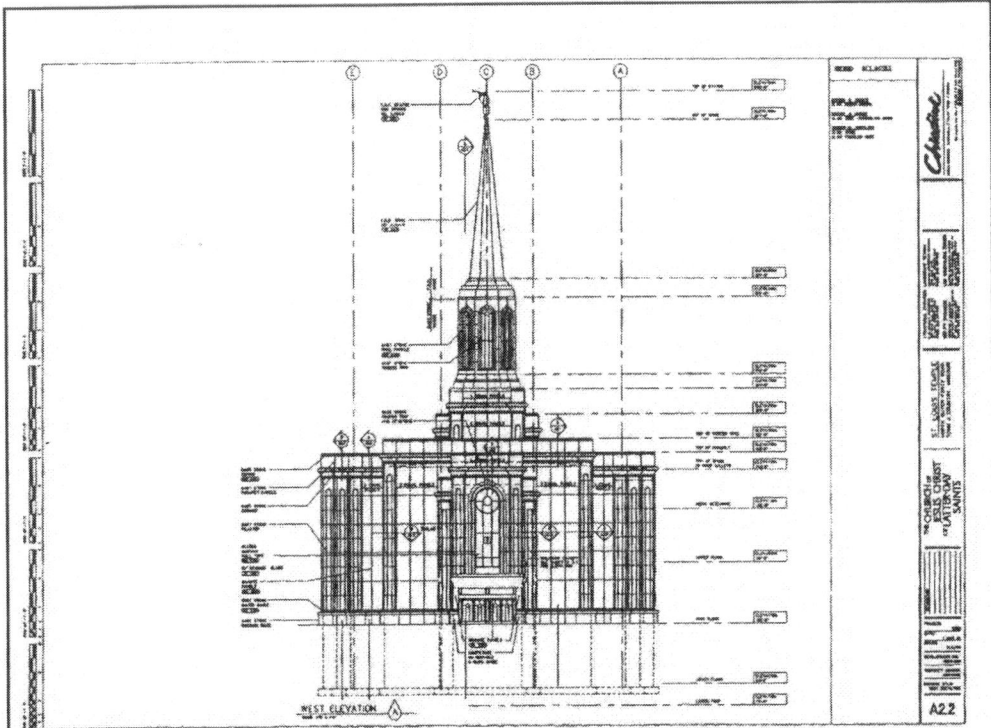

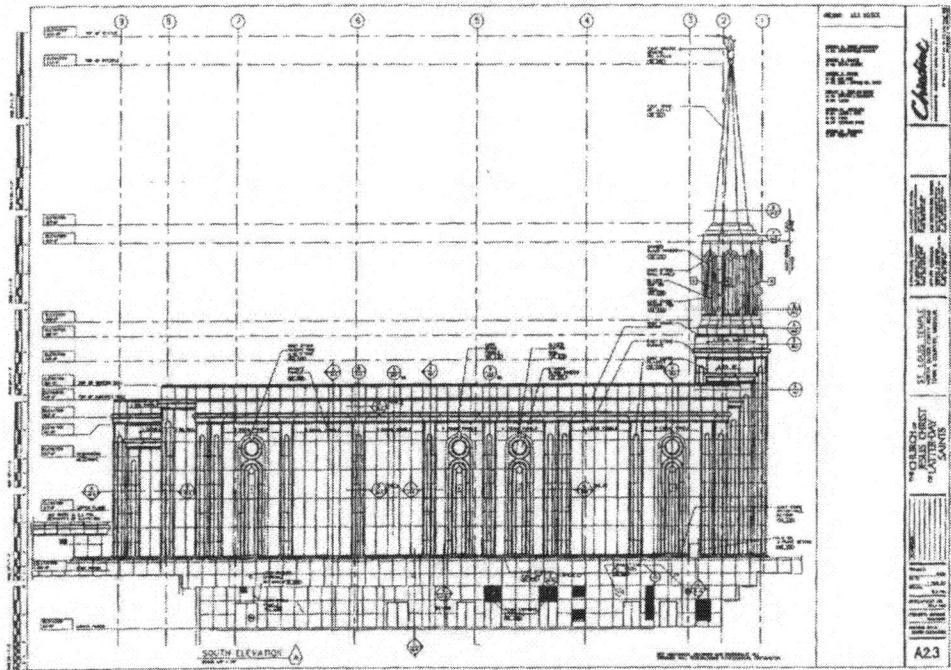

Chiodini Associates Architectural plans.

As tours were under way, Louis Chiodini, of Chiodini Associates, has commented that there have been only positive remarks about the temple. Especially significant were the compliments received from the City of Town and Country,
which has been previously noted as a tough critic.

After the November 1993 groundbreaking, site work began immediately, however, foundation work was postponed until Spring for warmer weather.
Construction of the temple didn't actually begin until almost two years later, in
late March, 1995.

Design of the temple was under the direction of Robert Dewey of the Temples and Special Projects Department. Local architect was the firm of Louis Chiodini and Associates. Construction was supervised by Gary Holland. General Contractor was the firm of BSI Constructors, headed by Joseph Shaunessey.

Principal events and dates in the process of construction included the following:

- Water main boring under U.S. Highway 40 began June 1, 1994 by J & J Boring Inc.
- Sanitary & Storm sewers began June 1, 1994 by Karsten Equipment Co.
- Notice to proceed given to BSI Constructors, Inc October 31, 1994.
- First footing concrete poured January 26, 1995.
- Main floor deck pour June 13, 1995.
- Millwork received from Fetzers of Salt Lake City May 22, 1995.
- Roofing installation began October 5, 1995.
- Angel Moroni installed (1st attempt) March 15, 1996.
  Completion on March 18, 1996.
- Turnover to Temple Department April 19, 1997.

The result is a magnificent House of the Lord situated on a promontory over-looking one of the area's major highways with 130,000 cars passing by each day. Not only are the members pleased with the building but the entire community has been impressed and has taken great pride in this landmark structure. Its beauty and prominence have no doubt accounted for the great outpouring of people who came to visit the building have remarked enthusiastically about the striking design, the impressive white granite exterior, the beautifully landscaped grounds and the elegant interior with its impeccable craftsmanship and unsurpassed quality of equipment, furnishings and decor.

If the members of the temple district succeed in building their lives as impressively as the temple has been built, then truly they will be ready to usher in Zion in St. Louis.

President Gordon B. Hinckley views construction progress during visit on April 15, 1995. Top photos left to right: viewing basement and foundation. Middle left: Lowell Hardy, Secretary to Pres. Hinckley, Gary Holland, Project Superintendent, Pres. Hinckley, Menlo F. Smith, Vice Chairman Temple Committee. Middle right: Pres. G. Richard Oscarson, St. Louis Stake, Pres. Hinckley, Menlo F. Smith. Bottom left: View of excavation. Bottom right: Menlo F. Smith, Gary Holland, Pres. Hinckley

Views of various stages of construction progress.

Statue of Angel Moroni is finally in place and granite cladding is complete

Designing temple can be daunting job

The job of designing the mammoth Mormon temple went to Chiodini Associates, a Clayton-based architectural firm.

Few architects have the opportunity to work on a building of this size and significance, so the firm was pleased to be chosen, said Louis Chiodini, president.

"I don't know of many buildings in the St. Louis area that have the same kind of image and projection that this building has," Chiodini said.

When it was commissioned to design the building, Chiodini Associates was presented with drawings of other Mormon temples, Chiodini said.

Most of those temples had a Southwestern design, though, and weren't appropriate for the St. Louis temple, so architects started from scratch, he said.

Design work began in November 1992, and a team of six to eight architects, headed by Steve Hermann, worked on the project.

The architects enjoyed working with the Mormons, Chiodini said, because of the importance placed on the temple building.

"We had to do some understanding of how they approached the various aspects of the building from a religious standpoint," Chiodini said. "We took this project very seriously."

The importance of temples means building them for the use of many generations. Temples are constructed to last at least 300 years, said G. Richard Oscarson, president of the St. Louis stake.

This requirement was one of the challenges in designing and building the temple, Chiodini said. Because it had to exceed standard seismic guidelines, certain materials had to be used.

Limestone and marble were unsuitable, because they are too brittle and porous to fit the standards the church required, Chiodini said. Instead the outer walls of the church were constructed of white granite.

The firm's projects have varied from religious to corporate to academic, and the firm has now been chosen to design Mormon temples being built in Nashville and New York, Chiodini said.

— Allyson McCollum

ST. LOUIS POST-DISPATCH, MISSOURI APR. 1997

Angel Moroni in place.

SAINT LOUIS MISSOURI TEMPLE

SIZE

The temple has approximately
60,000 square feet of floor space.

SPIRE

The spire rises to 150 feet, including the
gold-leafed statue of the Angel Moroni.

EXTERIOR

The exterior of the temple is white granite and
cast stone, which is enhanced by art glass windows.

INTERIOR

Celestial Room, four ordinance rooms, four sealing
rooms, a baptistry, offices, cafeteria and laundry.

LANDSCAPING

The temple site is enclosed by an attractive six-foot
decorative iron fence with a sage green patina. The
grounds are beautified with grass, trees, shrubs,
flowers and a water fountain.

SECTION THREE

one • PREPARING FOR THE OPEN HOUSE

*A*s the construction of the Saint Louis Temple advanced, the great task of setting forth plans for the open house began to take shape. Under the direction of chairman, Menlo F. Smith and the Temple Committee, an army of more than 6,000 faithful members were called to fill the many positions needed. Committees were formed to handle the thousands of ticket requests, the *Hosanna!* newsletter, printing, distribution, training, a speakers bureau and media. Stakes were asked to provide ushers, security, parking attendants, cleaning, organists, choirs, and sewing as well as volunteers for other positions.

Temple Open House Committee left to right and back to front: Richard Baier, Chester Miller, R. Grant Rees, Gail Uzelac, Derek Metcalfe, Stuart Preece, Shirley Stucki, Joseph Gossett, Verner Stromberg, Boyd F. Schenk, Menlo F. Smith, Neil Lewis, Fred Farmer, Donald Wolff, Kay Reeve Wierda, Gary Holland, Dale Wagstaff, Ronald Recker, Preston King, John Hardy, Larrie Christensen, Doug Clark, David Jensen, Don Wallace, David Dayhuff, Jean Mathews.

TEMPLE OPEN HOUSE COMMITTEE

CHAIRMAN
Elder H. Burke Peterson•Elder James M. Paramore
Elder William R. Bradford•Elder Hugh W. Pinnock

VICE CHAIRMAN
Menlo F. Smith

AUDIO/VISUAL
Don Wallace

CORNERSTONE/DEDICATION COORDINATOR
Grant Rees

GROUND BREAKING COORDINATOR
Roy W. Oscarson

HOUSING & ACCOMMODATIONS
Robert Gurr•Verner Stomberg

INFORMATION BOOTH
Rand Olsen

MUSIC
Larrie Christensen

OPEN HOUSE COORDINATOR
Fred Farmer

PUBLIC AFFAIRS
Jean Matthews•Keith Sawyer

PARKING & TRANSPORTATION
Doug Clark

STAFFING & TRAINING
Preston King

SECURITY
Richard Kearsley•Jospeh Gossett

TICKETING & PRINTED MATERIALS
Kaye Reeve Wierda

USHERS
Chester Miller

VIP/PUBLIC TOURS COORDINATOR
Boyd Schenk

TEMPLE SUBCOMMITTEE MEMBERS

Gary Holland Construction Superintendent

Richard Baier Exec Secretary

Ron Recker Treasurer & Budget

Paul Jarvis • Tanya Jarvis • Courtney Walker Temple History

AUDIO/VISUAL COMMITTEE

Chairman Don Wallace

Mike Benne • John Mathew • Walt Nichol • Don Saunders

CORNERSTONE/DEDICATION COMMITTEE

Coordinator R. Grant Rees, Sr.

Dennis Coleman • Phil Crain • Michael Downey • Arden Drysdale • Lester Farrell •
Joe King • Neal Lewis • Mike Longwel • Jim Mears • Tom Oram • Sherry Ree •
Fred Shepherd • Dennis Silva • Cal Squires • Don Wolff

HOUSING & ACCOMMODATIONS COMMITTEE

Chairman Verner Stromberg

INFORMATION BOOTH COMMITTEE

Chairman Rand Olsen

Chuck Healy • Newell Jensen • Karvel Kofoed • Gene Motley •
Shane Neifert • Duane Powell • Vicki Preece

MUSIC COMMITTEE

Chairman Larrie Christensen

Claudine Barner • Michael Belnap • Jannet Brown • Brent Carruth •
Brent Christensen • Larrie Christensen • Stephanie Cooper • Ron Dowse •
Shanna Duke • Kelly Egan • Greg Farmer • Brian Felt • George Fuhriman •
Pat Fuhriman • Lisa Grotts • Miava Helsloot • Caroline Hemming • Jessica Hill •
Patti Hintze • Paul Hintze • Marilyn Huntsman • Suzanne Kitchen • Donnia Krebs •
Kay Lewis • Danna McDaniel • Jenie Metcalf • Carolyn Morgan • Marsha Mortensen •
Victor Olvera • Valerie Peck • Marlyse (Marcy) Petersen • Susan Pomeroy • Bonnie Quigley •
Mary Alice Rapp • Thomas Royal • Amy Sawyer • Christine Schuman • Phyllis Senzee •
Anne Smith • Bonnie Terrell • Carla Williams • David Willis • Joan Wooley

OPEN HOUSE COMMITTEE
Coordinator Fred Farmer
Jack Dolen•Tom Farmer•Melvin O. Gadberry•Nile D. Griffiths•Brian Highfill•Matthew Jensen•James T. Johnson• Stephen Johnson•Fred Kitchen•Donald L. Mayfield•Kenneth Munk•Thomas Murphy•Jon Schaumann•Dean Tiffany•Jack Witbeck

PUBLIC AFFAIRS COMMITTEE
Chairman Jean Mathews
Jennifer Eliason•Larry Ficklin•Jana Flake•Ryan Frost• Ann Hartley•Newell Jensen•David Keetch•Pui Yan Kwok•Brad Lewis•Jeanette Mahaffey•Shannon Mahaffey•John Mathews• Randy Olsen• Linda Oscarson•Gary Otis•Evan Pedersen•Kristi Petersen•Randall Pope• Keith Sawyer•David Sylvester •Myra Sylvester•Charles Taylor•Ronald Watters

SECURITY COMMITTEE
Chairman Joseph Gossett
Lamar Capener•Chuck Clemins•Dana Farnsworth• Layne Flake• Mike Koplin•Wayne Mayer•Jim Miller•Tom Noble•Dr. Steve Oliver•Scott Pulley•Mike Sisson•Farrell Sorenson• Brian Vliett•Russell Watters

STAFFING AND TRAINING COMMITTEE
Chairman Preston King
Kevin Andersen•Michael Bartlett•Mark C. Blackwell•F. Greg Burton•C.S. Claybrook•Gordon Cotton•Michael Dorff• Ken Gerald •Robert L. Hartin•Ron L. Herrick•Jack Kyamey• Ron Lanfer•Don Little•Dan McClean•Bro. Mathhews•Earl Nail• Blaine Plamer•Alan K. Passey•Gary Pedersen•Lloyd Shirley•J. David Stocker•John Temple•David Thomason•Ferrol Truman• Gail Uzelac•Christine Woodbury

TICKETING AND PRINTED MATERIALS COMMITTEE
Chairman Kaye Reeve Wierda
Dale Adams•Carolyn Barnard•Joan Stopa-Beecroft•Mark C.

Blackwell•F Greg Burton•Elizabeth Chipman•Murel Cobb•Sarah Cox•
RaeJean Crandell•Darrel K. Danielson•Jack Davis•Michael Dorff•
Steve Drown•Flint Finlinson•Jane Flint•Ken Gerald•Robert Goodrich•
Sue Hansen•Kim Harris•Mark Harris•Paul Jarvis•Tanya Jarvis•
Ronald Herrick•Keith R. Kappes•Eric Kartchner•John Knutti•
Sharon Kunzelman•John Knutti•Pat Larkin•Joseph A. Leister•
Margaret Lohrum•John Mills•Thomas Nelson•Joanna Nicklin•
Lee Noe•Alan K. Passey•Verl T. Pope•Jeffery L. Raleigh•John C. Reid•Mary
Reynolds•Suzanne Shepherd•Scott Sucher•Elaine Sullivan•Cindy Taylor•Diana
Taylor•David Thomason•Liz Welch•
Ester Wheat•Brenda Willis•John Willis•Amanda Yancey

TRANSPORTATION AND PARKING COMMITTEE

Chairman Doug Clark

John Boyd•Dirk Burton•Ed Calhoun•Loren Chapman•Dave
Cortez•Jeff Divis•Duane Eberhardt•Duane Evans•Jim
Flake•David Goodman•Dave Hansen•Morris Hardisty•Doug
Hartin• Rick Kercher•Richard Lewis•Gary Long•John Lunceford•
Robert Maddox• Basil Nolan•Randal Pope•Bill Popp•Gary
Robinson•Jim Tschudy•Andy Weeks•William Wiles

USHERS COMMITTEE

Chairman Chester Miller

Cheryl M. Basnek•Burt Bergeron•Austin Bonnett•Teddy Church•
J. Neill Clugston•Jime Daniel•Darrel K. Danielson•Ken Davidson•
Bobby Dowell•Boyd Evans•Larry Faria•Robert Ferwalt•Robert Gibson•
Dennis Hartin•Ron Heilig•Phil Hickman•Patriarch Hubert Hinds•John Kipp•
Bill McCord•Leroy McKinney•Robert Maddox•Ray Miller•Michael Morris•Reid
Mortensen•William Morter•Royd Nelson•Eric Radichel•Michael Ree•Fred Shepherd•
Byron Taylor•Darwin Thompson•Joseph Tsai•Jim Wilson•Larry Woodbury

VIP/PUBLIC TOURS COMMITTEE

Chairman Boyd Schenk

David Jensen•Loretta Jensen•Susan Nelson•Carolyn Renfro•
John Stucki•Shirley Stucki•Bonnie Wehrmeister•Joyce Wolff

ST. LOUIS MISSOURI TEMPLE

OPEN HOUSE

APRIL 26 - MAY 17

Monday 8:00 am - 7:00 pm   Tues-Sat 8:00 am - 9:00 pm   Closed Sunday

"HOSANNA" NEWSLETTERS

BANNER

TICKET

NAME BADGES

Tour the New St. Louis Temple

Open to The Public From April 26 - May 24

To reserve a time call 314-827-9330 8 a.m. - 8 p.m. Monday - Friday

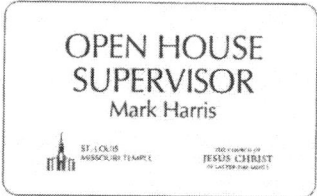

THE CHURCH OF
JESUS CHRIST
OF LATTER-DAY SAINTS

OPEN HOUSE INVITATION

ST. LOUIS MISSOURI TEMPLE

Thank you for your quiet reverence.

SIGNAGE

73

On the following pages are just a small sampling of articles from various newspapers across the country, reporting on the opening of the St. Louis Temple.

Open House for St. Louis Missouri Temple

The more than five million members of the Church of Jesus Christ of Latter-day Saints ("Mormons") residing in the United States will soon see the long-awaited completion of the St. Louis Missouri Temple, which was begun in 1992. Church leaders have recently announced that the open house for the public will begin April 26 and will continue through May 17, 1997. The St. Louis Missouri Temple will be the 50th operating temple of the church and will serve nearly 100,000 Church members throughout Kentucky, Tennessee, Missouri and large portions of Indiana, Illinois, Nebraska and Kansas, including the approximately 75 members in Ohio County.

"We are truly excited about the completion of the St. Louis Temple and feel that it will be a great blessing to the members living in this area. We want to invite our friends, neighbors and the public to

visit and tour the building during the open house period," said Blaine Pieper, President of the Hartford Branch.

The St. Louis Missouri Temple is of importance to Church Members in Western Kentucky because temples are considered the most sacred buildings on earth. Presently, the nearest temple is in Atlanta. Members of the Church of Jesus Christ of Latter-day Saints believe marriages conducted in the temples of the Church are eternal in nature and that families united in temple ceremonies will be linked together throughout eternity. The temple will be dedicated in June after which it will be open only to members of the church in good standing.

Temples are closed on Sundays so church members can attend and participate in Sunday worship services in their regular chapels. Tours of the new building will be

conducted beginning at 9:00 AM each day and will continue until 9:00 PM except on Mondays, when tours will end at 7:00 PM. Members of the public may obtain tickets to

participate in an open house tour through local church leaders or by calling Marianne Pieper at 274-3960, or call toll free 1-800-595 5392.

St. Louis Missouri Temple

TIMES- NEWS, KENTUCKY JAN. 1997

Photo submitted

Temple open house set

The more than five million members of The Church of Jesus Christ of Latter-day Saints in the U.S. will soon see the completion of the St. Louis, Mo., Temple, begun in 1992. Church leaders recently announced open house for the public will be April 26-May 17. The temple will be the 50th operating temple of the church and will serve nearly 100,000 church members throughout Missouri, and large portions of Indiana, Illinois, Kentucky, Tennessee, Nebraska, Kansas and Arkansas, including the approximately 450 church members in the Mountain Home area. Tours of the new building will be conducted from 9 a.m.-7 p.m., except Mondays, when tours will end at 7 p.m. There will be no tours on Sundays. Members of the public may obtain tickets to participate in an open house tour through local church leaders or by calling 425-7744, 424-2006 or (800) 595-3392.

Temple offers open house

The Church of Jesus Christ of Latter-day Saints is offering a once-in-a-lifetime opportunity for people to see its beautiful new St. Louis Missouri Temple, which is located not far from the intersection of Highway 40 and Interstate 270.

The church will hold a three-week free open house from April 26-May 17. Tours will include a video, an exhibit and a guided tour. After the temple is dedicated, only members of the church in good standing will be able to enter the building.

Hours will be 9 a.m.-7 p.m. Monday and 9 a.m.-9 p.m. Tuesday-Saturday. Reserve tickets at (314) 827-9430 after March 15. ■

St. Louis temple doors open to public in April

The First Presidency has announced the public open house and dedication dates for the St Louis Missouri Temple, now nearing completion on a 14-acre site in the St Louis suburb of Town and Country.

Public open house of the edifice will be April 26 through May 17, except Sundays. The temple will be dedicated in 11 sessions June 1-3 to allow as many worthy Latter-day Saints as possible within the 80,000-member district to attend. Included in the temple district are Missouri, parts of Nebraska, Kansas, Illinois, Indiana and Arkansas.

When dedicated, the temple will be the Church's 50th operating temple and the 26th in the United States. Ground was broken for the building on Oct. 13, 1993.

Temples nearing completion are in Preston, England, and Vernal, Utah. Others under construction are in Bogota, Colombia; Guayaquil, Ecuador; and Madrid, Spain. Temples for which ground has been broken are in Cochabamba, Bolivia, and Recife, Brazil. Temples announced are in Billings, Mont.; Boston, Mass.; Caracas, Venezuela, Monterrey, Mexico; Nashville, Tenn.; and White Plains, N.Y.

LDS CHURCH NEWS   JAN.11, 1997

FRIDAY, JANUARY 31, 1997

Local Mormons prepare for opening of new temple

By CANDICE HAMMOND
Staff Writer

The St. Louis Church of Jesus Christ of Latter-day Saints Temple is nearing completion, according to a spokesperson.

It will be the 50th operational temple for the church. Groundbreaking on the three-floor, 59,000 square-feet building, which is located on a 14-acre plot of land 20 miles west of the Mississippi River in the City of Town and Country, took place on Oct. 30, 1993. The exterior of the temple is constructed of white granite and precast stone, with a single, 150-feet tall spire topped off by gold-leafed statue of the angel Moroni.

According to the spokesperson, as spectacular as the building is to view, it has an even more extraordinary meaning to the over 100,000 church members in Missouri, Arkansas, Kansas, Illinois, Nebraska, Kentucky, Tennessee and Indiana, served by the structure—of which approximately 450 members reside in the Mountain Home area.

The temple is not to be a place for regular Sunday worship, but rather reserved for special family-oriented rituals, such as marriages and dedications, according to Mountain Home Latter-Day

Photo Submitted

Saints Public Affairs Director Jilleen Darracq.

Darracq said that the Latter-Day Saints (Mormons) teach that any couple married in one of their temples will be joined permanently in the bonds of marriage throughout eternity.

According to Darracq, the church's doctrine also states that any child born of such a marriage may be brought to the temple and "sealed" together with their families so that they may remain a complete family in the hereafter.

The Saint Louis Temple will be open for tours to the public from April 26 through May 17, after which it will remain open only to members of the church. Tours will be conducted daily from 9 a.m. to 9 p.m., except on Mondays, when end at 7 p.m. Tickets for the tours may be obtained through local Latter-day Saints leaders, or by calling 501-425-7744, 501-424-2006 or 1-800-595-5392.

■ The new Mormon temple here will be open to the public for three weeks this spring. After May 17, it will close forever to non-Mormons.

By Patricia Rice
Post-Dispatch Religion Writer

For three weeks this spring, St. Louis Mormons will open the doors of their new St. Louis Missouri Temple to the public.

"We hope as many as 200,000 people take tours," said Jean H. Mathews, a Mormon spokeswoman and a former state representative from Florissant. Tickets are required.

It's a one-time only invitation.

Doors will open to the public April 26, then close forever to non-Mormons on May 17. Once a Mormon temple is formally dedicated, only Mormons with special recommendations by their bishops may enter. For instance, non-Mormons may not attend weddings at the temple.

The gleaming white, marble-faced temple has become a landmark just north of Highway 40 (Interstate 64) and west of Interstate 270. The temple is the first Mormon temple in Missouri.

In 1958, about 2,000 Mormons were in the state; today, 12,000 live in the St. Louis area alone. The temple will also serve about 80,000 additional Mormons, including those in Missouri, Kansas, southern Indiana, Southern Illinois, western Kentucky and western Tennessee.

The temple will be formally dedicated June 1-3. The building will become the 50th operating temple in the world. The building cost more than $18 million.

Temples are the most sacred buildings to Mormons, who use them only for special activities — not for Sunday worship. According to Mormon theology, marriage ceremonies conducted in a temple are eternal in nature. Families whose members are joined in temple ceremonies — called ordinances — will remain united throughout eternity, Mormons believe.

Mormons from ages 12 to 18 will spend weeks in the temple baptistery performing "proxy baptisms" on the dead.

In April, people with tickets will be led through many of the 100 rooms in the 58,749-square-foot building. The culmination of the tour will be the celestial room with a 24-foot, domed ceiling. Visitors can walk only on plastic runners that lightly adhere to the golden, hand-sculpted Wilton carpeting. Women in high heels must wear booties to prevent the heels from puncturing the plastic.

"It would cost $1 million to replace the carpeting," Mathews said.

Tours will be from 9 a.m. to 9 p.m. Tuesdays through Saturdays, and from 9 a.m. to 7 p.m. Mondays. Temples are closed on Sundays. In addition to the temple's 240 parking spaces, two neighboring churches and several business will open parking lots to visitors. Buses will shuttle visitors from lots to the temple.

When requesting tickets, state the number of tickets desired, dates preferred and whether you prefer day or evening. Include name, address and phone number. Large groups may reserve a specific hour. Tickets may be ordered by calling (314) 838-6257, or by writing to: St. Louis Temple Committee, 510 Maryville College Drive, Suite 210, St. Louis, Mo., 63141. Tickets will be mailed in March.

The St. Louis Missouri Temple just north of Highway 40 and west of Interstate 270.

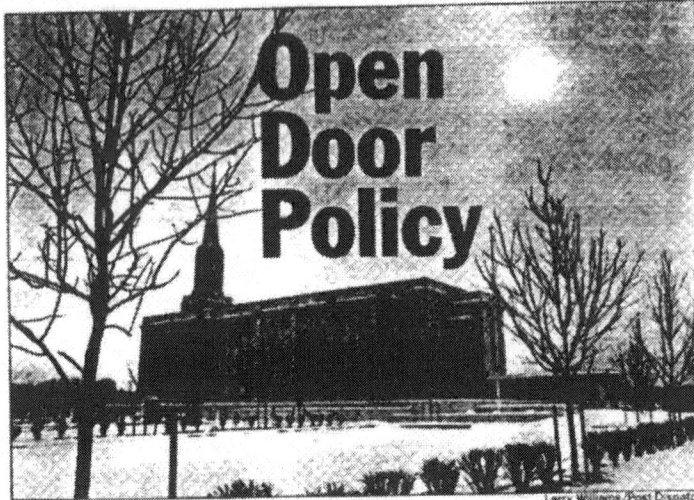

Larry Williams/Post-Dispatch

February 5, 1997   WEST NEWSMAGAZINE

Temple Nears Completion, Open House Set

Upon its completion, the St. Louis, Missouri Temple of the Church of Jesus Christ of Latter-day Saints will serve more than 2,000 members of the Church who reside in West County.

Church leaders have announced a public open house beginning April 26 and continuing through May 17. Free public tours will be conducted from 9 a.m. to 7 p.m. on Mondays and from 9 a.m. to 9 p.m. Tuesdays through Saturdays. No tours will be given on Sundays.

The St. Louis, Missouri Temple, the 50th operating temple of the Church, will serve more than 12,000 members in the metropolitan area as well as an additional 80,000 members throughout Missouri, and large portions of Indiana, Illinois, Kentucky, Tennessee, Nebraska and Kansas.

"We look forward with great anticipation to the completion of this beautiful house of the Lord and to inviting our friends, neighbors and the public to view the building during the open house period," said G. Richard Oscarson, president of the St. Louis Stake and a resident of West County.

The St. Louis, Missouri Temple is of importance to church members in the Midwest because temples are considered the most sacred buildings on earth. Presently, the nearest temple is in Chicago. Members of the Church believe marriages performed in their temples are eternal in nature and their families joined in temple ceremonies will remain united throughout eternity.

After dedication in June, the temple will be open only to members of the Church in good standing. The building will be closed on Sundays so church members may attend and participate in regular Sunday services in their own chapels.

The temple is located on North Outer Forty Drive, one-third mile west of Hwy. 270. For more information and reservations, call 256-6762.

'Sacred place' open to public for one month

Mormons with permission allowed in after dedication

By Allyson McCollum
Staff writer

It became a landmark before it was completed.

Perched on a hill and topped with the gold figure of an angel, the temple for The Church of Jesus Christ of Latter-day Saints has not gone unnoticed. Already about 200,000 people have signed up for the chance to walk inside the stone edifice, off Interstate 64 (Highway 40) west of I-270.

Temples are considered by the Latter-day Saints, also called Mormons, to be the most sacred place on earth, said Jean Mathews, regional public affairs director for the church. As such, building or entering them is no simple matter.

Prior to the temple's dedication, it will be open to the public for one month. Once dedicated to God, it will be closed to all but church members who have permission to enter.

Permission comes as a result of personal interviews with a bishop and the stake president, to determine if the member is living according to the church's teachings, said G. Richard Oscarson, president of the St. Louis stake.

A stake is a unit of organi-

zation of the Mormon Church. There are nine congregations in the St. Louis stake.

Probably about 90 percent of

Tours offered; tickets needed

Tours of the The St. Louis Missouri Temple of The Church of Jesus Christ of Latter-day Saints will run April 26 through May 24, from 9 a.m. to 7 p.m. Mondays, and 9 a.m. to 9 p.m. Tuesdays through Saturdays.

There is no charge to tour the temple, and donations will not be accepted but tickets are required.

Call 821-6703 for tickets or information.

Prior to entering the temple, visitors will see a short video explaining the purpose of temples. Once inside, the tour is self-guided, though there are audio recordings and signs to explain the purposes of different rooms. Volunteers will be available to answer questions.

— Allyson McCollum

most congregations have earned permission to enter a temple, Oscarson said, though it may be less in some because of the stake's proximity to a temple.

The St. Louis Missouri Temple of The Church of Jesus Christ of Latter-day Saints is only the 50th Mormon temple in the world. It will serve between 90,000 and 100,000 people in portions of eight states, Mathews said. Until now, Mormons in St. Louis have had to travel to Chicago for temple ceremonies.

After successful interviews, members receive a certificate to present upon entering a temple. Interviews are repeated once a year, Oscarson said.

Membership and the activity

See TEMPLE Page 10A

Towering temple

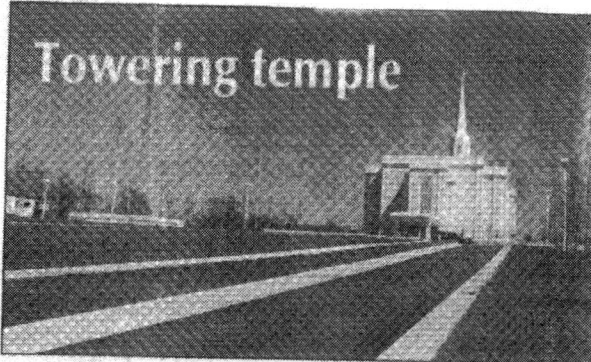

Rick Graetz/photos

The St. Louis Missouri Temple of The Church of Jesus Christ of Latter-day Saints is one of only 50 Mormon temples in the world. It is located on Interstate 64 (Highway 40) west of I-270.

Mormon Temple Open House Scheduled April 26 thru May 24

St. Louis Missouri Temple

by Jeannine Dahlberg

Church construction has reached its apogee in the St. Louis Missouri Temple for the Church of Jesus Christ of Latter-day Saints which dominates a hilltop along Highway 40 in Town and Country. The combination of white Bethel granite and cast stone is a favorite for ecclesiastic architecture. The formidable, magnificent structure casts a brilliance of purity with the trumpeting angel, Moroni, atop the steeple heralding it is a "house of the Lord."

The trumpeting angel will beckon guests only once to visit the sacred Mormon temple. Tours will be available from April 26 through May 24, from 9:00 a.m. to 7:00 p.m. on Monday; and from 9:00 a.m. to 9:00 p.m. on Tuesdays through Saturdays; May 19 through May 24, 5 p.m. to 9 p.m. only.

Call 827-9430 for reservations.

St. Louis Temple completion near

Evansville, Indiana -- The more than five million members of The Church of Jesus Christ of Latter-day Saints (Mormons) residing in the United States will soon see the long-awaited completion of the St. Louis Missouri Temple, which was begun in 1992.

Church leaders have recently announced that the open house for the public will begin April 26 and will continue through May 17, 1997. The St. Louis Missouri Temple will be the 50th operating temple of the Church and will serve nearly 100,000 Church members throughout Missouri, and large portions of Indiana, Illinois, Kentucky, Tennessee, Nebraska and Kansas, including the 2,500 church members in the Evansville, Indiana Tri-State area.

"We look forward with great anticipation to the completion of this beautiful house of the Lord and to inviting our friends, neighbors and the public to visit and tour the building during the open house period," said James W. Hansen, President of the Evansville Stake (diocese) of the Church.

The St. Louis Missouri Temple is of importance to Church members in the midwest because temples are considered the most sacred buildings on earth. Presently, the nearest temple is in Chicago. Members of The Church of Jesus Christ of Latter-day Saints believe marriages conducted in the temples of the Church are eternal in nature and that families united in temple ceremonies will be linked together throughout eternity. The temple will be dedicated in June after which it will be open only to members of the Church in good standing.

Temples are closed on Sundays so Church members can attend and participate in Sunday worship services in their regular chapels. Tours of the new building will be conducted beginning at 9:00 a.m. each day except Sunday and will continue until 9:00 p.m. except on Mondays, when tours will end at 7:00 p.m. Members of the public may obtain free tickets to participate in an open house tour through local church leaders or by calling 338-6665 or 812-471-0191.

Mormon temple

A rare peek inside for outsiders

By Teri Maddox
Belleville News-Democrat

TOWN AND COUNTRY, Mo. — Boyd K. Packer, president of the Church of Jesus Christ of Latter-day Saints, knows that some people will tour the new St. Louis Missouri Temple and think Mormons have strange beliefs and practices.

Visitors will see health-club-style dressing rooms, where church members change into white robes before ordinance work (leads to confirmation). The temple has no large sanctuary, only chapels and other small rooms for religious study, prayer and ceremony.

These include four sealing rooms, where couples marry for eternity (a step beyond the "till-death-do-you-part" civil promise). Only families are present, and only if they are church members.

The circular baptismal font rests on the backs of 12 lifesized fiberglass oxen, representing the 12 tribes of Israel. A computer screen displays genealogical records as church members are being baptized vicariously for their dead ancestors.

"We're not so anxious, I suppose, to have everybody agree with us as we are to have them understand us," said Packer, 72, the third highest-ranking Mormon leader. "If they'll stop to understand us, then they'll see that it's the church of Jesus Christ. We worship Christ. He's our redeemer. We preach the same doctrine that's in the New Testament."

Packer was in St. Louis this week to open the new Mormon temple, the 50th in the world. It sits on a 14-acre tract in the suburb of Town and Country along U.S. 40 (about 45 minutes from Belleville).

More than 200,000 people are expected to tour the temple in the next month, starting today. Admission is free, but reservations are required (call 800-595-5392). After the dedication in early June, only Mormons in good standing — those who are moral, faithful, temperate and committed to family — will be allowed inside.

There are nearly two dozen LDS churches in the St. Louis metropolitan area. But for the past 10 years, members have had to travel to the temple in Chicago for eternal marriages and ordinance work. Before that, they went to Salt Lake City or Washington, D.C.

The St. Louis Temple was built to serve about 93,000 Mormons who reside in Missouri, Southern Illinois and parts of five other Midwestern states. But church leaders expect visitors from all over the world.

The church has named St. Louis businessman Merlo F. Smith, 70, to the unpaid position of temple president. He was chairman of Sunmark Capital Corp. (a candy farm he founded in 1952) until several years ago when it was purchased by Nestle. He now is in the investment business.

His wife, Mary Jean Jacobson Smith, 70, will serve as temple matron. The couple will supervise 15 paid employees and hundreds of volunteers. Besides religious facilities, the temple has a cafeteria, laundry and garden.

"We have no professional clergy as such in the church," Packer said. "All members of the church are expected to live the gospel of Jesus Christ, and we're expected to be responsible in our family."

For people of the Mormon faith, temples are sacred places where they have a direct link to God and their ancestors. That is why the church spares no expense in building large, majestic structures with lavish facilities and furnishings.

The St. Louis temple, designed by the local architectural firm Chiodini Associates, cost more than $18 million. The general contractor was BSI Contractors.

The three-story exterior is white granite and precast stone. A 150-foot spire is topped by a 12-foot gold-leaf statue of the angel Moroni, prophet of the Book of Mormon. The 59,000

square-foot interior features tall columns, art-glass windows, rotunda ceilings, crystal chandeliers, gold-framed mirrors and fabric flower arrangements. Most furniture, wall coverings and carpet are off-white or ivory colored.

Most artwork shows scenes from Mormon history or Jesus in traditional Biblical settings. However, a painting in the cafeteria has him preaching to Native Americans, a concept that is described in the Book of Mormon and unique to the Mormon faith.

"As you go through the temple, you'll find it's as beautiful as we know how to make it with the resources that we have," Packer said, noting that the temple was financed by church members, through donations and tithes (weekly contributions of 10 percent of income).

Construction of a temple for the Church of Jesus Christ of Latter-day Saints in Missouri has special significance. In the 1830s, Mormons were persecuted and banished from the state (under an "extermination order" by the governor) because of their religious views.

Soon after, church members founded the city of Nauvoo, Ill., but they were driven out there, too. Leader Joseph Smith was killed by a mob. In 1847, his successor, Brigham Young, led a trek across the plains to Salt Lake City, where the church still is headquartered. Thousands died under harsh conditions.

At a press conference this week, Packer told reporters that his Danish great-grandmother made the trip, pulling a handcart. She bought three pairs of shoes in St. Louis, wore two out and walked barefoot through parts of the Rocky Mountains to save the third pair for her arrival in Salt Lake City. But her feet were so swollen and bloody she could not put on the shoes.

Today, the Church of Jesus Christ of Latter-day Saints has about 10 million members worldwide. It also commands an army of 55,000 missionaries, mostly young, single men, who pay their own way for two years of service.

"I suppose, in simple terms, all we're about is fixing it so that a man and his wife and their children can be happy at home and live a worthy life, to make a contribution to the community, make a contribution to the church, be examples of plain, Christian, decent living," said Packer, the father of 10. "We do a lot of praying. The church is directed by revelation. We move as we're directed to move."

"(The church) will grow, with or without a temple," he added. "That's true everywhere in the world. It'll grow very rapidly. People who are unsettled and looking for stability and looking for the fundamental doctrines of the gospel find it. ... We're ordinary people, but there's something that we have to offer that's nowhere else. The gospel speaks for itself."

BELLEVILLE NEWS DEMOCRAT

Public viewing available for St. Louis Temple, new area landmark, for limited time

St. Louis' newest landmark, The St. Louis Missouri Temple of The Church of Jesus Christ of Latter-Day Saints, is found overlooking Highway 40 in St. Louis County, just west of I-270.

The structure is remarkable for its dramatic setting and its exterior of white granite and pre-cast stone, and its spire reaching 150 ft. above the ground; topped by a 10 ft. tall gold leaf statue of an angel with a trumpet.

The building is three floors and nearly 60,000 sq. ft. situated on 15 landscaped acres.

This will be the 50th operating temple constructed by the Church throughout the world and the first in Missouri, serving nearly 100,000 members of the Church throughout Missouri and surrounding states.

Unlike numerous chapels of the Church in the St. Louis area and throughout the world, temples are religious instruction and other ceremonies.

The Temple will be dedicated in ceremonies beginning June 1, 1997, and continuing for several days. After the dedication, only members of the Church in good standing will be admitted to the building. For several weeks preceding the dedication, a special Open House event will be held, allowing the public the opportunity to tour the building.

The Open House for the public will begin April 26, and continue through May 17. The hours are from 8 a.m. to 9 p.m. weekdays and Saturdays, except Mondays, when it will close at 7 p.m. The Temple will be closed on Sundays. Individuals or groups interested in attending the Open House can obtain reservations by calling 314/827-9430.

ST. LOUIS LAWYER, MISSOURI   APR. 1997

ST. LOUIS MISSOURI TEMPLE - Pictured above is the new St. Louis Missouri Temple for members of The Church of Jesus Christ of Latter-day Saints, "Mormons", which will be serving nearly 100,000 church members.

Open House Announced For St. Louis Missouri Temple

The more than 17,000 members of The Church of Jesus Christ of Latter-day Saints, "Mormons," residing in the Illinois and Missouri bi-state area will soon see the long-awaited completion of the St. Louis Missouri Temple, which was begun in 1992. Church leaders have recently announced that the open house for the public will begin April 26 and will continue through May 17. The St. Louis Missouri Temple will be the 50th operating temple of the church and will serve nearly 100,000 church members throughout Missouri, and large portions of Indiana, Illinois, Kentucky, Tennessee, Nebraska, and Kansas, including the 135 church members in the Macon area. The temple is located 1/3 mile West of I-270 on Outer North Forty Drive in the city of Town and Country in St. Louis County.

The St. Louis Missouri Temple is of importance to church members in this area because temples are considered the most sacred buildings on Earth. Presently, the nearest temple is in Chicago. Members of the Church of Jesus Christ of Latter-day Saints believe marriages conducted in the temples of the church are eternal in nature and that families united in temple ceremonies will be linked together throughout eternity. The temple will be dedicated in June after which it will be open only to members of the church in good standing.

Temples are closed on Sundays so church members can attend and participate in their regular chapels. Public tours of the new building will be conducted beginning at 9 a.m., Monday through Saturday, and will continue until 9 p.m. except on Mondays, when tours will end at 7 p.m. Tickets for the open house may be obtained through local church leaders or you may call 1-800-595-5392.

"We look forward with great anticipation to the completion of the temple and to inviting friends, neighbors and the public to visit and tour the building during the open house period," said John C. Jorgensen, President of the Columbia Stake (diocese) of the church.

NEW TEMPLE: Artist's conception of the new facility.

Temple to open in April

By Teri Maddox
Belleville News-Democrat

In the 1800s, members of the Church of Jesus Christ of Latter-day Saints (Mormons) were persecuted and banished from Missouri because of their religious views.

Next month, a majestic new Mormon temple — the 50th in the world — will open in the St. Louis suburb of Town and Country, off U.S. 40 just west of Interstate 270.

"This particular temple has a special meaning to people because it is the first truly Midwest temple," said Jean Mathews, director of public affairs for the St. Louis Missouri Region, home to about 15,000 Mormons.

There are nearly two-dozen LDS churches in the St. Louis metropolitan area. But for the past 10 years, members have had to travel to the temple in Chicago to participate in sacred ceremonies. Before that, they went to Washington, D.C.

Ceremonies include "marriages for eternity" and baptisms for the dead (living family members serve as proxies).

The baptismal font at the St. Louis temple — identical to the one in Salt Lake City — is patterned after the "golden basin" of Solomon's temple in the Old Testament. It is mounted on the backs of 12 gold-leaf oxen, representing the 12 tribes of Israel.

"It is very striking," Mathews said. "The oxen are life-sized, so it's a very large, very imposing structure."

The exterior of the three-story, 60,000-square-foot temple is white granite and precast stone. A 100-foot spire is topped by a 12-foot, gold-leaf statue of the angel Moroni.

According to church history, it was Moroni who provided Mormon founder Joseph Smith with the golden plates from which he translated the Book of Mormon in the late 1820s.

Besides the baptistry, the interior of the temple includes a celestial room, ordinance and sealing rooms (for marriages), chapels, offices, a cafeteria and service and maintenance facilities. Landscaping will blend into woods on the 14-acre property.

After dedication of the temple, only LDS members in good standing will be permitted inside. Before the dedication, an open house will be held for the public. Reservations are required.

Originally, the open house was scheduled for April 26 through May 17. But church leaders have considered extending that by a week.

"There's been an explosion of interest in the project," Mathews said. "We already have over 50,000 requests for tours of the building. It took us all by surprise."

To request a reservation, write the Temple Committee, Church of Jesus Christ of Latter-day Saints, 510 Maryville College Drive, Suite 210, St. Louis, MO 63141.

BELLEVILLE NEWS-DEMOCRAT, ILLINOIS MAR. 1997

'Overwhelming' Interest Extends Open House At Mormon Temple

By Patricia Rice
Post-Dispatch Religion Writer

So many St. Louisans want to see the new St. Louis Temple of the Church of Latter Day Saints that its open house is being extended a week. Now, it will be open from April 26 to May 24. And the doors will open an hour earlier than planned — from 8 a.m. to 9 p.m.

"It's overwhelming, more than we ever expected. We probably will have 300,000 visitors," said Jean H. Mathews, a church spokeswoman and former state representative from Florissant. When she announced the open house in January, she expected 200,000.

The white, marble-clad building north of Highway 40 (Interstate 64) and west of Interstate 270 in Town and Country has drawn attention throughout its construction. After its dedication in June, it will be closed to all but Mormons in good standing.

The guided tour will take about 40 minutes, Mathews said. Visitors may see the main rooms in the 100-room, 58,749-square-foot building. To protect the carpet, women wearing high heels will not be allowed inside.

Reservations are required. Call 827-9430 or (800) 595-5392 between noon and 8 p.m. Monday through Friday. Tours are not offered on Sunday.

ST. LOUIS POST DISPATCH

LOCAL/NATIONAL CHURCH NEWS

Rolla Mormons excited about St. Louis Temple

The more than five million members of the Church of Jesus Christ of Latter-day Saints ("Mormons") residing in the United States will soon see the long awaited completion of the St. Louis Missouri Temple, which was begun in 1992. Rolla is home to a congregation of the church.

Church leaders have recently announced that the open house for the public will begin April 26 and will continue through May 17. The St. Louis Temple will be the 50th operating temple of the church and will serve nearly 100,000 church members throughout Missouri, and large portions of Indiana, Illinois, Kentucky, Tennessee, Nebraska and Kansas.

The St. Louis Temple is of importance to church members in the Midwest because temples are considered the most sacred buildings on earth. Presently, the nearest temple is in Chicago. Members of the Church of Jesus Christ of Latter-day Saints believed marriages conducted in the temples are eternal in nature and that families united in temple ceremonies will be linked together throughout eternity. The temple will be dedicated in June, after which it will be open to members of the church in good standing.

Temples are closed on Sundays so church members can attend and participate in Sunday worship services in their regular chapels. Tours of the new building will be conducted beginning at 9 a.m. each day and will continue until 9 p.m. except on Mondays, when tours will end at 7 p.m. Members of the public may obtain tickets at no charge, although they are required to participate in an open house tour and may be obtained through local church members or by calling (314) 827-9430. Directions for the St. Louis Temple are Highway 40, west of 270 at Mason Rd.

St. Louis Temple

SATURDAY/April 26, 1997

COMICS/TV
Pages B-6,7

The Salt Lake Tribune

Religion

St. Louis LDS Temple Stirs Up Interest

BY SAMUEL AUTMAN
SPECIAL TO THE TRIBUNE

TOWN AND COUNTRY, Mo. — The LDS Church is about to open its 50th worldwide temple in Missouri, the state where in 1838 many pioneering Mormons were attacked, some died and another 12,000 fled at gunpoint.

The St. Louis Missouri Temple, actually located in a prosperous suburb 15 miles west of downtown St. Louis, will serve about 80,000 Mormons in Missouri, southern Illinois, Kansas, Nebraska, western Kentucky, western Tennessee and southern Indiana.

The Church of Jesus Christ of Latter-day Saints' first Missouri temple will be formally dedicated in ceremonies June 1-3, after which it will be open only to Mormons in good standing. Menlo F. Smith, a St. Louis businessman, has been appointed president of the temple, and his wife, Mary Jean Jacobson Smith, will serve as matron. From now until late this week in May, visitors can tour the temple.

Jean H. Mathews, an Ogden native, is the church spokeswoman and a former state legislator in the St. Louis area. When the *St. Louis Post-Dispatch* ran a short story last January announcing that the temple would be open to non-Mormons for tours in April and May, she expected a few hundred inquiries.

Within one week, her family received 1,000 phone calls at her residence, some from as far away as Vancouver, Wash.; Toronto, Tampa, Fla. and San Diego. Nearly 200,000 free tickets have been distributed, and Mathews expects more than a quarter of a million people to visit it in the 30-day period.

"It shows that there have been a lot of people who have heard about Mormons, both negative and positive," Mathews said. "They recognize this is an opportunity to see if what they have heard is true."

When Mathews was a lawmaker in the early 1980s, she spent much of her time at the State Capital in Jefferson City debunking myths about Mormons. People wondered if racial minorities could be church members, what kinds of strange ceremonies happened in Mormon temples and if Mormons are polygamous.

"I am often asked how many wives my husband has. I look at them and say, 'He can't even handle one,'" Mathews said.

The first settlement of Mormons in Missouri

LDS Temple In St. Louis Stirs Up Interest

■ Continued from B-1

took place in 1831, just a year after the church had been established in New York. Mormon founder Joseph Smith designated Jackson County in western Missouri as the location of the millennial Zion, or New Jerusalem, and as the gathering place for the Saints.

Thousands of members gathered in Independence, Mo., and

...wave of converts from New England, Canada and the British Isles.

But the swelling number of Mormons alarmed non-Mormon settlers, who viewed them as strange and religiously unorthodox. Local Protestant clergy also felt threatened by zealous proselytizing among their flocks by Mormon missionaries. As transplanted Southerners, many Missouri residents were slaveholders who feared that the Yankee Mormons would incite their slaves to revolt.

Armed conflict between the Mormons and their Missouri neighbors soon erupted. By 1838, hostilities were so intense that Gov. Lilburn Boggs issued an "extermination order" giving Mormons 30 days to leave Missouri or risk being attacked by the militia. Within two years, 12,000 had fled. From 1841 to 1855, St. Louis was a major stop for thousands of Mormons on their way to a Mormon colony in Nauvoo, Ill., and later on their way to Salt Lake City.

But the Latter-day Saints never forgot Missouri. To this day, the faithful believe that Independence is the site of the valley where Adam and Eve had lived. It is to this place that Mormons believe they will return when Christ comes again to the earth at the millennium. It commands a mythic and doctrinal place in the Mormon imagination.

Richard Oscarson, president of the St. Louis stake, moved to the area in 1943, when he was a little boy. There were 200 active members in the city at the time, and in his view, seeing Mormonism move from near obscurity to opening a temple is nothing short of miraculous.

Today there are 12,000 members in St. Louis, and 40,000 in the entire state.

Until 1973, Mormons from the Midwest had to travel to Salt Lake City for temple functions. With the opening of the Washington, D.C., temple in 1974, the distance was cut in half. When the Chicago temple opened in 1985, members were relieved to only have a 5-hour car trip from St. Louis.

"Now it will only be a 10-minute drive," said Bishop Pui Kwok of the Lindell Ward in St. Louis.

The St. Louis Temple has been long in coming. The church bought the land from the Missouri Baptist College in 1990. The gleaming white, marbled temple sits prominently on a hill north of U.S. Highway 40.

Some passers-by have assumed the 59,000-square-foot structure is part of the Baptist college.

"It's the same problem that would arise if it was a Lutheran chapel built next to a Greek Orthodox cathedral. People would assume there was some relationship," Mathews said. "I hope we continue to have a good relationship with the Baptists. I see no reason why we won't."

SALT LAKE TRIBUNE, UTAH APR. 1997

Earth tones, wrapped in white, with golden ceilings

300,000 visitors expected, in white shoe coverings

By Lori Sharn
USA TODAY

A rare look inside a Mormon temple

The Church of Jesus Christ of Latter-day Saints is holding a series of open houses in a new $18.5 million temple in suburban St. Louis. Officials expect more than 300,000 visitors. Once the temple is dedicated June 1, only church members will be allowed inside. Mormons go to temples to be married and to conduct formal ceremonies, such as baptisms for the dead. Temples are not places of regular Sunday worship or instruction. That takes place in local chapels.

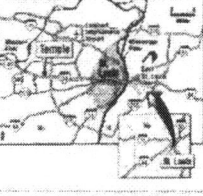

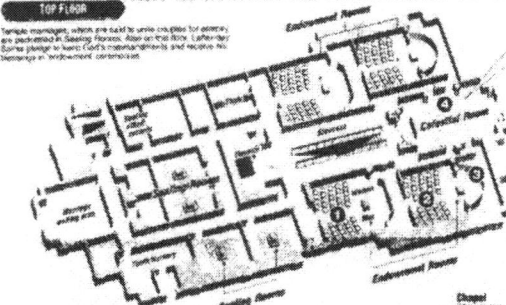

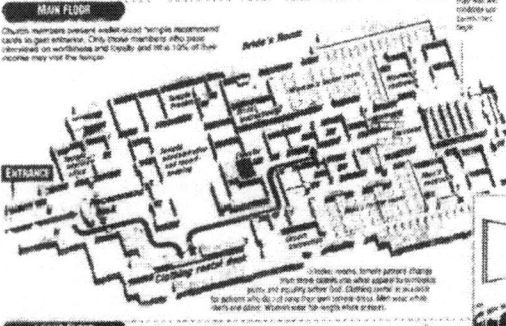

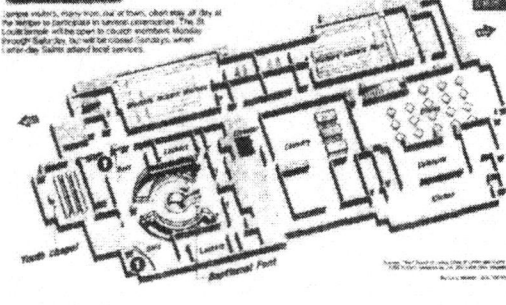

TOP FLOOR

MAIN FLOOR

LOWER FLOOR

THE ENDOWMENT CEREMONY

TEMPLE MARRIAGE

BAPTISM FOR THE DEAD

two • P U B L I C   O P E N   H O U S E

Church members had hoped for an enthusiastic response to their invitation to numerous dignitaries and to the public at large to visit during the open house for the St. Louis Missouri Temple. "We look forward with great anticipation to the completion of this beautiful house to the Lord and to inviting our friends, neighbors and the public to view the building during the open house period," said Richard Oscarson, President of the St. Louis Missouri Stake, in a news release announcing that everyone was invited to view the new temple.

The open house was scheduled for April 16 to May 17, 1997. No one was quite prepared for the response. Requests for open house tickets came in by the hundreds, then by the thousands and tens of thousands. Eventually requests reached almost 400,000, and a decision was made to extend the open house period one full week, to May 24. Sundays were also added by direction of the First Presidency to accommodate public request for open house tickets.

An army of thousands of members was required to fill positions as ushers, parking attendants and to perform other tasks. Stakes rushed to meet requests for supervisory and training personnel, as well as volunteers for other positions. Many members rearranged vacation time and others took time away from their employment. Some traveled from the far reaches of the temple district to serve.

Planning for the St. Louis Temple Open House began almost as early as the purchase of the site was completed and spanned a period of almost eight years. During this time four different Area Presidents served as the Chairman of the Temple Committee. Several of the Sub-committee Chairs changed during this time. Roy Oscarson, Coordinator of the Groundbreaking event passed away subsequent to that occasion but prior to completion of the temple. He had done more than perhaps any other individual to build the Church in the St. Louis area and thus make this temple possible. From the time of the announcement of the temple, his fondest dream was to see its completion but unfortunately this was not to be.

The open house required construction of an air conditioned pavilion tent just north of the temple building measuring 50' X 125' and consisting of a viewing area for a display portraying our temples and their purpose. It included a copy of the Christus statue by the famous Danish sculpture Thorvaldsen. The tent also housed two video viewing theaters used for showing an eight minute video film about temples. An additional video tent was subsequently constructed because public demand completely outstripped capacity.

The open house events were originally scheduled starting April 23 and concluding on May 17. However, the demand was so overwhelming that this was extended another week to May 24. A telephone center was established to handle reservation with 6 lines staffed 14 hours per day. This was totally inadequate from the beginning and was finally expanded to 15 lines. Before the open house ended almost 400,000 reservations were received.

Before the temple was opened to the public, three days of special VIP preview tours were held wherein over 5,000 distinguished visitors were hosted. These tours included notable leaders in business (181), government (129), education (22), religion (146), health care, law enforcement, military, law and media including:

> Governor Mel Carnahan of Missouri
> U.S. Senator Kit Bond of Missouri
> U.S. Senator John Ashcroft of Missouri
> U.S. Congressman James Talent of Missouri
> 200 + CEO members of Young Presidents Organization

Staffing the open house events required an estimated 6,000 volunteer members for the various positions, most serving at significant sacrifice. Many served on multiple occasions and would have gladly served again.

By the third week of the open house, attendance was well beyond 200,000 and seemed destined to exceed 300,000. Visitors were unanimous and enthusiastic in their praise and admiration for the beauty of the building and for the special spirit which they experienced during their tour. Missionary referrals reached record numbers.

Dignitaries visit St. Louis Temple Open House. Top left: Elder Boyd K. Packer; U.S. Senator Kit Bond; Menlo F. Smith. Top right: Elder Packer; Roger Wilson Lt. Governor of Missouri; Menlo F. Smith. Bottom left: Elder Packer; James Talent, U.S. Congressman Missouri 2nd Dist; Brenda Talent; Menlo F. Smith. Bottom right: Elder Boyd K. Packer, Acting President, Council of the Twelve Apostles; Mel Carnahan, Governor, State of Missouri.

"The temple is magnificent!"
-John Fox Arnold

"...truly enjoyed the tour and the hospitality extended. One of our group was wheel-chair-bound. From the time we arrived, the accommodations were outstanding. All of us were comfortable with all of the preparations. It is quite clear that the planning committee anticipated just about everything. The entrance through the tents provided opportunities to reflect on the nature of our visit, the videotape was helpful and the directions clear. Further, the team of ushers were excellent in insuring that we knew what to do and were able to do so in the most elegant manner possible.

...Now the citizens of St. Louis will be able to view the temple and be aware of the strength of your Church." -Peter E. Sargeant, Dean Webster University

"...it is awesome in every detail, and incredibly artistic and calming and functional and reverent.

...how to arrange it, how to control it and how wonderfully it was done was amazing.

But most of all, I would like to commend the hosts. As we progressed through each area, the people greeting us were warm, unassuming, willing, happy, proud, friendly, helpful, and comfortable with all of us aliens trouping through their hallowed territory.

The help you provided in donning (and removing) the booties was wonderful. The parking access and attendance, exemplary." -Beverly B. Price

"It truly is the most beautiful, sacred place! Also, we were very impressed at how nicely everyone treated us. Your young people are so neat and such high caliber people."
- Mrs. Pat Day For Monroe Country Homemakers Extension Group

"...I want to congratulate you on the volunteer infrastructure that clearly has contributed to the success of your opening. Every one of the volunteers with whom I had occasion to interact last night was not only polite and informative but also genuinely interested in helping!"

- Judy Studer, Executive Director, Civic Entrepreneurs Organization

"As our group assembled, Boyd visited with us and then escorted us into the tent for the preview video. It was informative and helped prepare us for the tour...Boyd was an excellent guide and was eager to answer all of our questions at appropriate times and we came away with a better understanding of the beliefs of the Mormon religion."

- Salem-in-Ladue Methodist Church Adult Sunday School Class

"You spoiled us -- all of the hosts were very pleasant, helpful and very cheerful. I was really pleased to see a wheelchair as we parked in the handicap. It was complete with "driver"...Your thoughtful group enabled Ben and me to enjoy everything...We came away feeling very good."

- Joan Edwards

"It was an experience we shall never forget. Learning about your faith was an added bonus. No wonder all of the members whom we know are such lovely people!"

- Turk and Janet Turley

"It was a wonderful experience to learn by seeing what the Jesus Christ we all believe in means to your denomination. Your "faithful" are to be commended on their hours of smiling and ushering."

- The Dorcas Group of Hamilton Christian Church - Judy Holscher

"It was truly inspiring and we deeply appreciate your letting us see it."

- Margaret R. Batchelor

"The temple is beautiful inside and out, and certainly a great addition to the St. Louis County scene. Many years of the best of wishes to you, an all attending members, of the temple."

- Florence C. Wehlage

"I had invited my 84 year old mother ...to take the tour. My mom said she needed to sit down. A gentleman asked if she would like a wheelchair...a Paul Bauer (Bower?) appeared with a wheelchair and got her seated and we all took the tour. We were treated beautifully and my mother really appreciated the help and attention...Paul is from Cape Girardeau, MO. He stayed with my mom, my son and me until my husband came with the car.

Although we are Roman Catholic...we ask God to bless all of you and your work. We thank you for the opportunity to tour the temple and for the kindness shown to us."
- Mary Clare Callahan

"You gave our family a delightful day with history, elegance and friendship."
- Betty G. Hopkins

"I am visiting here from Massachusetts. I was very much impressed...and the very warm and loving people who made everyone feel welcome...with the warm smiles on their faces...God bless them all...the feeling of peace and joy in seeing so many welcoming and warm faces to greet everyone...feel privileged to visit...may you all enjoy it for a long time to come. I had to have someone push me in a chair and the young man was very cheerful and polite. Every place I turned I saw beautiful and smiling faces welcoming us. I wish you all a good life and health in the name of our Lord Jesus and his father...all of my life of 86 years when I read the Bible I came to the words, 'Do unto others what you would like them to do unto you' I thought it was a grand thing and it appealed to me very much and I often wonder how wonderful it would be if we all lived that way."
-Mona Bezreh

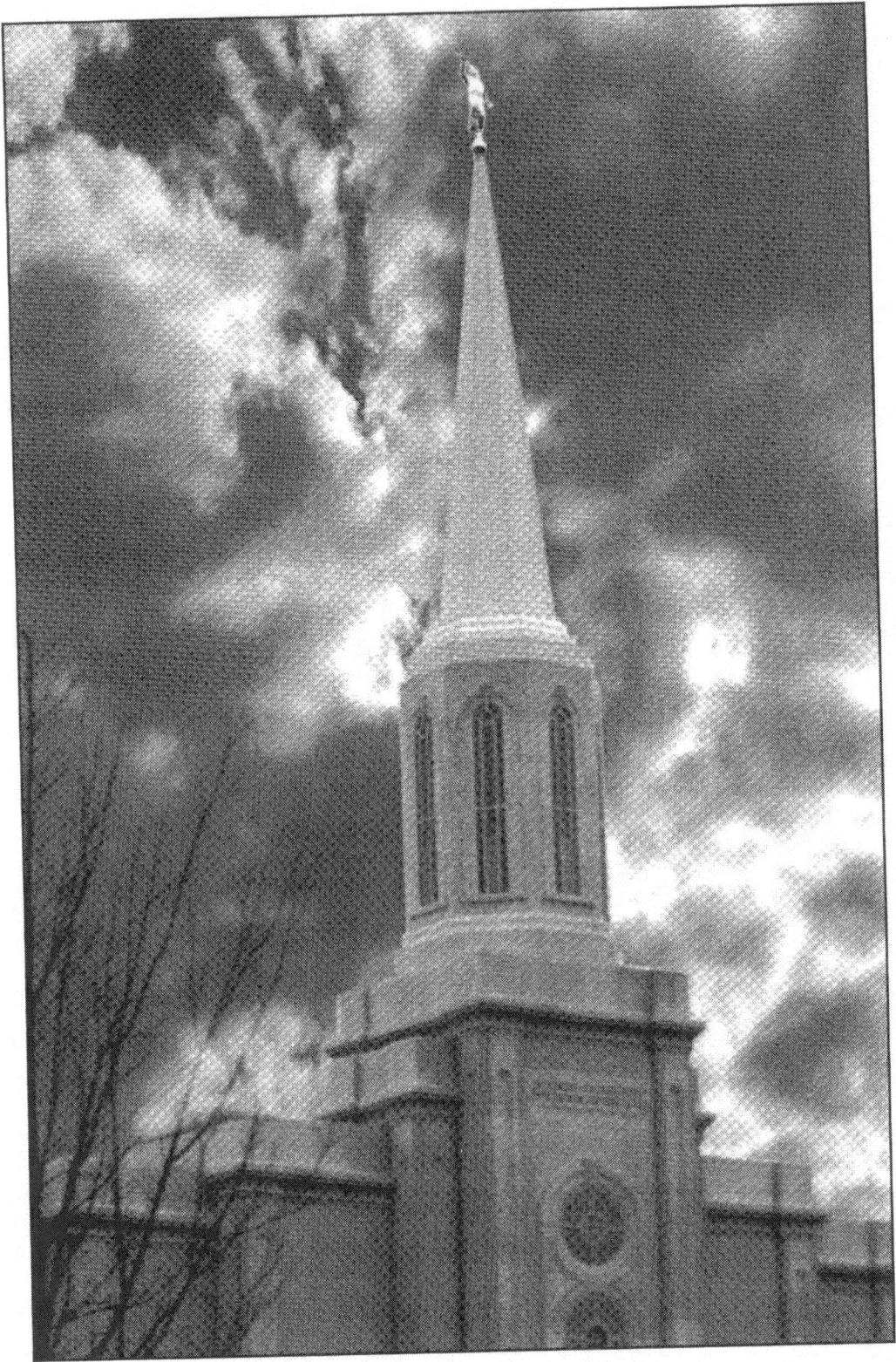

three • DEDICATION

The day that a temple would be dedicated in Missouri has been eagerly awaited by generations of Latter-day Saints. Excitement has grown all across the midwest as the time has grown nearer and the dedicatory dates for the St. Louis Missouri Temple were announced.

June 1-5, 1997

Members were notified that President Gordon B. Hinckley would preside as would President Thomas S. Monson and President James E. Faust. Other general authorities in attendance would include Elder Hugh W. Pinnock, Area President, and Elder W. Eugene Hansen, Director of the Temple Department for the Church.

Nineteen dedicatory sessions were scheduled, and up to 26,000 members were expected to attend. Plans were made to use the North St. Louis Stake Center as well, connecting it via closed-circuit television.

A sacred cornerstone ceremony preceded the first dedicatory session. Items placed in a cavity in the cornerstone included: a complete set of scriptures, newspaper editions, a copy of the *Ensign* magazine, this history book and other memorabilia.

A total of 19 dedication services for the St. Louis Temple were held starting on June 1, 1997 and running through June 5. The first service began at 8:00am on Sunday June 1st and included the Cornerstone ceremony. This session was presided over by President Gordon B. Hinckley who also presided at all sessions on Sunday and Monday. President Hinckley gave the dedicatory prayer for the first session as well as several others. President James E. Faust and President Thomas S. Monson shared the presiding duties at the sessions on Tuesday, Wednesday and Thursday June 3, 4 and 5.

Members of the Council of the Twelve attending and participating in the dedicatory sessions included Elders L. Tom Perry, David B. Haight, Russell M. Nelson, Dallin H. Oaks, Henry B. Eyring, and Robert D. Hales, all of whom were accompanied by their wives. Elders Hugh W. Pinnock, President of the North America Central Area and his counselors J. Richard Clarke and V. Dallas Merrell and their wives were also in attendance.

Elder W. Eugene Hansen, Executive Director of the Temple Department, was in attendance with his wife. Also representing the Temple Department was Derek Metcalfe, Manager of the Temple Department as well as John E. Hardy, Open House Coordinator.

Choirs from the 32 stakes comprising the St. Louis Temple District participated. A combined choir of Young Adults from the St. Louis area participated in the Cornerstone ceremony which was filmed and aired by local television.

Approximately 26,000 members attended the dedication with seating in all rooms of the temple as well as in the Temple Ancillary Building. The culminating event of each session was of course the traditional Hosannah Shout.

Top left: The baptismal font and baptistry area. Top right: Sealing room. Bottom left: Bridal room. Bottom right: Waiting area near the front entrance of the temple. Opposite page: The Celestial Room.

four • TEMPLE PRESIDENCY

Menlo F. Smith of the Frontenac Ward, St. Louis Missouri Stake, has been called by the First Presidency as president of the St. Louis Missouri Temple. His wife, Mary Jean Jacobson Smith, will serve as temple matron.

President Smith is well known both in Church and business circles throughout the St. Louis Region, and continues to serve as vice chairman of the St. Louis Missouri Temple Committee. Those who know him say they were gratified but not surprised by his call as temple president.

"Obviously we're honored to receive this call," President Smith said. "We're excited about it and grateful that we'll have the opportunity to participate in the affairs of this new temple."

He said he asked President Gordon B. Hinckley, who extended the call, about juggling the duties of Temple Committee Vice Chairman and his other responsibilities with those of his new calling. President Hinckley was already well aware of those circumstances, President Smith said with a chuckle. "Characteristically, he replied by saying, 'Oh, just carry on.'"

A convert to the Church, President Smith was baptized at age 42. "Strangely enough I grew up in Salt Lake City as a non-member," he said. "I had no interest in the Church until some 20 years after coming to St. Louis."

Like many who have joined the Church, he attributes the beginning of his testimony to having felt prompted to begin reading the Book of Mormon. Though he was happy and successful before, "My life has been wonderfully better ever since," he said. President Smith, now 70, has been a mission president and counselor, regional representative, regional public communications director, high counselor, bishop and Sunday School President. He was born in St. David, Arizona, son of J. Fish and Lillian Fountain Smith.

Sister Smith graduated from the University of Utah. She served with her husband in the Philippines Baguio Mission and is a former Relief Society President, counselor and instructor and held other teaching positions in the auxiliaries. She was born in Tonopah, Nevada, to Rufus Ingman and Marvel Gardener Jacobson. President and Sister Smith have five children and 12 grandchildren.

Boyd F. Schenk of Town and Country, Missouri, has been called as first counselor in the presidency of the St. Louis Missouri Temple. His wife, VerLee, will be an assistant to the matron.

Brother Schenk, High Priest Group Leader in the Frontenac Ward in the St. Louis Missouri Stake, is a former president of the St. Louis Stake and former bishop. He is a retired president and chief executive officer of Pet Inc.

R. Don Oscarson of Phoenix, Arizona, has been called as second counselor in the temple presidency. His wife, Shirley, also will be an assistant to the matron.

Brother Oscarson is a son of the late Roy W. Oscarson, who pioneered the reestablishment of the Church in the St. Louis area. He is former bishop, former counselor in the St. Louis Missouri Stake and former president of the Milwaukee Wisconsin Stake.

Menlo F. and Mary Jane Smith

Boyd F. and Verlee Schenk

R. Don and Shirley Oscarson

ST. LOUIS MISSOURI TEMPLE STAFF

Temple President Menlo F. Smith
1st Counselor Boyd F. Schenk
2nd Counselor R. Don Oscarson
Temple Matron Mary Jean Smith
Assistant to Matron Verlee Schenk
Assistant to Matron Shirley Oscarson

ADMINISTRATIVE STAFF
Temple Recorder David B. Dayhuff
Assistant Recorder Gail Uzelac
Ordinance Clerk Bradley Wheeler
Secretary Judith Waidmann
Clerks Carolyn Popp • Larrie Christensen • Kristina Rondot

BUILDING, GROUNDS, CUSTODIAL STAFF
Building Engineer Dale Wagstaff
Building Staff Lon Chesley • Jack Howe • Robert Arbogast
Grounds Richard Rahm • Anita Osborne • Robert Boyer
Custodial Luis Correa • James Ford • Gary Wierzbicki • Robert Wachob •
Brenda Moore • Susan Dixon

SECURITY STAFF
Security Supervisor Scott Scharffs
Officers Wes Blank • Arnold Jensen • David Oland • Cory Van Horne

CLOTHING STAFF
Supervisor Arvilla Finlayson
Staff Luther Pattillo • Nancy Strawderman

CAFETERIA STAFF
Supervisor Lee Reeder
Cooks Therese Sawyer • Virgina Hopkins• Lafi Manumaleuna

SECTION FOUR

one • SAINT LOUIS AREA HISTORY

*S*ituated on the west bank of the Mississippi River, about 10 miles south of its confluence with the Missouri River, St. Louis in its early days was nick-named "Mound City" because of its prehistoric Indian mounds, even after those were leveled as the area was settled and its population began to expand.

A mission to the Indians had been established on the site in 1700, but was abandoned three years later. When it was selected in December 1763 by New Orleans trader Pierre Laclede and his stepson Rene Auguste Chouteau for construction of a trading post, it was in Spanish Territory, although the population was predominantly French.

In 1780, during the American Revolution, St Louisans aided by a garrison of Spanish soldiers resisted a British attack that was aimed at cutting off the American colonists' trade on the Mississippi and Ohio rivers. Napoleon acquired the area from Spain in 1800, then sold it to the United States in 1803 as part of Jefferson's famed "Louisiana Purchase." It was a United States Territory until 1811 when Missouri became the nation's 24th state.

St. Louis was incorporated as a village in 1808 and chartered as a city in 1822. In a new state constitution passed in 1876 the city was granted "home rule" status, enabling it to operate as both city and county.

For many years, St. Louis was the nation's largest fur trading center. It also was the starting point for military, scientific and exploratory expeditions west, the most famous of which is the Lewis and Clark Expedition of 1806. The first Mississippi River steamboat reached St. Louis in 1816 and river traffic grew steadily until the Civil War. Large numbers of emigrants, including many Latter-day Saint converts, traveled up the Mississippi to St. Louis by steamboat. There they found work, enabling them to purchase supplies and equipment for their journey west to Oregon, California or Utah.

In 1849 a fire that started on a steamboat moored on the riverfront spread ashore, destroying thirteen city blocks. St. Louis suffered another setback that same year when a cholera epidemic killed a fifth of its population.

Rail lines reaches St. Louis in 1852 and the area's first bridge across the Mississippi was constructed by James B. Eavs. In 1860 the outbreak of the Civil War found Missourians deeply divided in their views. Missourians voted not to secede from the Union, but sympathy for the South was strong in much of the populace. For four years, conflicts ran deep and often erupted in violence. There were many battles and hundreds of skirmishes, although St. Louis avoided much of the fighting as its citizens attempted to continue their trading and manufacturing, most of which supported the North.

After the Civil War, the area's economy and population grew rapidly. A major highlight was the Louisiana Purchase Exposition, now better know as the World's Fair of 1904.

World War I brought more industrial expansion. That slowed in the Great Depression of the 1930s, but reached new heights during World War II from 1940 to 1945, with the aircraft industry beginning to take the lead. By 1970, the city of St. Louis was no longer among the nation's 10 most populous, but it continued to be a major center for barge, railroad and air transportation.

Prominent St. Louisans have included Charles Lindbergh, Joseph Pulitzer, Eugene Field, Marianne Moore and T.S. Eliot. Author Samuel Clemens (Mark Twain) worked in the St. Louis printing trade.

As of the 1990 census, St. Louis had 396,600 residents, down from more than 800,000 in the early part of the century, but the surrounding metropolitan area which includes three adjoining counties in Missouri and three in Illinois exceeded two million. Germans form the largest ethnic group, but there are substantial communities of Irish, Italians, African-Americans, Poles and others. From its earliest settlement, the area's predominant religion has been Roman Catholic, but many other religions are represented, the largest of which are Lutherans and Southern Baptist. St. Louis has been consistently more tolerant of differing religious viewpoints than much of its surrounding area in Missouri and Illinois.

Sites of interest include Forest Park (site of the 1904 World's Fair), the world-class St. Louis Zoo, the St. Louis Art Museum, the Old Court House where the Dred Scott Decision was handed down, the Old Cathedral, the Cahokia Mounds State Historic Site in nearby Illinois, the Jefferson National Expansion Memorial, and the world-famous Gateway Arch.

two • SAINT LOUIS CHURCH HISTORY

*J*uly 2, 1978, is a unique day, not only in the 147 year-old history of the Saints in St. Louis, but in the history of the Restoration. Spencer W. Kimball is the first President of the Church ever to return to a city where he labored as a missionary and dedicate a chapel built by the Saints. We present today will be telling this experience to our children and grandchildren as those who lived in St. Louis in 1915 and 1916 have told us about meeting President Kimball when he was here as a missionary.

St. Louis has been a city of pioneers as surely as any other city in our history, for a pioneer is someone who goes before, preparing the way for others. The purpose of this memorial program is to honor properly those urban pioneers who have made today possible and also those pioneers here today who will bring to pass a greater future for this stake.

Among us at this time are a few of the old pioneers who remember the lean years when the Church met in a renovated meat market on Easton Avenue. Others remember the Maple Avenue Chapel. In our midst are many who were present at the end of World War II who resolved that the time had come to build a chapel of their own, a full Church program, and somehow once again become a stake. Still more present saw those dreams realized when twenty years ago, on June 1, 1958, the second St. Louis Stake was organized. The whole story of the Saints in St. Louis is a story that becomes increasingly more dramatic and interesting as we follow it from the beginning to the present.

During most of the nineteenth century, St. Louis was the hub of trade and culture for the great western waterway system of the upper and lower Mississippi, Ohio, Missouri, and Illinois rivers. Founded by the French in 1764, St. Louis was, by the time the Mormons first visited it, a sixty-seven year old settlement, a nine year old city – a young giant destined to become the "Fourth City" of our country by the end of the century. Throughout the Missouri and Illinois periods of the Church, up to the coming of the railroad to Utah in 1869 and beyond, St. Louis was the most important non-Mormon city in Church history.

It became not only an oasis of tolerance and security for the Mormons, but a self-sufficient city never fully identified or connected with rural Missouri or with nearby Illinois – areas it considered backward and inferior. This is one reason why St. Louis never condoned nor participated in the Missouri and Illinois persecution of the Mormons.

St. Louis played two important roles in early Mormon history – as a city of refuge and an emigrant center. As a large and tolerant city, it gave protection to Mormons in the 1830s when they fled persecution in western Missouri and to the refugees from Illinois mobs in the mid-1840s. The first wave of convert-emigrants from Europe passed through the city in April 1841, and until at least 1855 the main route for thousands of European converts to Nauvoo, Illinois, and later to Utah, was via St. Louis.

Although the history of the Church in early St. Louis is episodic and the sources scanty, many interesting and important events took place there. Almost every major Church leader of the period was connected with the Church in St. Louis. There were the Prophets and Apostles: Joseph Smith, Brigham Young, Heber C. Kimball, John Taylor, Parley P. Pratt, Sidney Rigdon, Oliver Cowdery, Martin Harris, Frederick G. Williams, Willard Richards, Charles C. Rich, Franklin D. Richards, Ezra Taft Benson, George A. Smith, Erastus Snow, Abraham O. Smoot, Orson Pratt, Jedediah M. Grant, Orson Hyde, Orson Spencer, Amasa Lyman, and Moses Thatcher.

Other interesting and important events connected with the early Church in St. Louis include the publication of William Clayton's *Emigrants' Guide*, the establishing of a Mormon newspaper, the *St. Louis Luminary*, public solicitations to aid destitute Mormon exiles, the organization of a lyceum, the organization of the first stake outside of Utah, the exhibiting of Joseph Smith's Egyptian mummies, papyri, Kinderhook plates, and the casting of the font of type for the Deseret Alphabet.

The Church in St. Louis grew from a small colony to a large stake which included all or parts of five states - Missouri, Illinois, Iowa, Indiana, and Kansas Territory. Its early history can be conveniently divided into the following periods: the Colony, 1833-1843 the Branch, 1844-1847; the District, 1847-1854; the first Stake, 1854-1857 (discontinued); an interim century, 1858-1957; and the second Stake, 1958-1978.

THE COLONY, 1833-1843

Less than one year after the organization of the Church on April 6, 1830, the first Mormons passed through St. Louis, in obedience to a commandment (Doctrine and Covenants 28) to take the gospel to the Lamanites on the western frontier. Consequently, in October 1830, Parley P. Pratt and four missionary companions, left Fayette, New York, on foot for western Missouri. Sometime during January 1831, they crossed the Mississippi on a ferry to the foot of present-day Market Street, and headed west, still on foot, via St. Charles Independence, Missouri. During the short layover in St. Louis and vicinity, they did some preaching and made some friends, if not converts.

Later that year in June, Joseph Smith and others passed through St. Louis en route to Independence. The Prophet walked to Independence via the famous Boonslick Road which passed right by today's St. Charles Ward Chapel. He was soon followed by the whole Coleville, New York Branch of about sixty members which stayed in St. Louis during June 13-18, before proceeding to Independence on a boat up the Missouri. In 1832 Joseph Smith again passed through en route to Independence, and Parley Pratt was there several times.

By 1833, as a result of missionary activity and Missouri mobs, there was a small group or colony of Mormons in St. Louis. Throughout the rest of the decade St. Louis received formal visits from missionaries.

In 1858 the St. Louis press began to take some notice of the Mormon question. (I have collected 690 references to the Mormons in the St. Louis press for the period of 1859-1848 alone.) On November 8, for example on troubles in the western part of the state, and on December 20, the *St. Louis Daily Evening Gazette* briefly reported the Missouri Argus expressed sympathy for the Mormons and their sufferings.

During the subsequent expulsion of the Mormons from Missouri throughout the winter of 1838-1839, a number of leading newspapers in St. Louis supported the Mormons and condemned Governor Lilburn W. Boggs. Such efforts did the Mormons of western Missouri no good, but it may be one reason why no Mormons in St. Louis were expelled. Some of the citizens of St. Louis held meetings to raise funds to assist the destitute exiles.

Soon after the removal of the Mormons to Nauvoo, Illinois the results of the British Mission (opened in 1837) were felt in St. Louis. The first emigrant group passed through in April 1841. Throughout the Nauvoo period, and up to 1855, the emigrants came up the Mississippi from New Orleans to St. Louis where it was necessary to change boats to continue on the upper Mississippi to Nauvoo. While most of the converts proceeded to Nauvoo as quickly as possible, some stopped over in St. Louis for a variety of reasons – the main one was to work and recoup their finances. Over the years so many Mormons worked in St. Louis that in 1855 the *St. Louis Luminary* (a Mormon newspaper) of February 3, 1855 reported: St. Louis is a fine, large, and flourishing city, and has furnished employment to many hundreds and thousands of our brethren ... there are few public buildings of any consideration in this city that our brethren have not taken an active and prominent part in erecting or ornamenting. There are few factories, foundries, or mercantile establishments, they have taken, or are taking an active part in establishing or sustaining. Consequently the colony prospered. There was also some missionary activity on the Illinois side of the river in Madison and St. Clair counties.

THE BRANCH, 1844-1847

Apparently it was during the spring of 1844 that the first formal branch of the Church was organized in St. Louis. In that same year one of the earliest stories appeared in the St. Louis press about local Mormons. On May 16 the *People's Organ* reported, "We understand that a few of the followers of Holy Joe have located themselves on Morgan (now Delmar) St. and hold forth in the school house every now and then." A week later the branch was visited by Brigham Young, Heber C. Kimball, and perhaps 100 other elders. This sudden influx from Nauvoo was the result of Joseph Smith's decision to campaign for the presidency of the United States.

To stump for him Joseph called about 350 able-bodied men to spread throughout the country. Brigham Young and his group arrived in St. Louis on May 22.

There they called the Church together and instructed them both religiously and politically. Heber C. Kimball recorded in his journal that about 300 were present. On the 23rd, the group sailed for Cincinnati and the East.

Instead of being elected, Joseph was assassinated June 27, 1844 and the St. Louis press printed many stories condemning this murder. Typical of the attitude regarding this event is the following statement from the *St. Louis Evening Gazette* of July 1: "THE MURDER OF THE PROPHET: It was Murder -- Murder of the most deliberate, cold-blooded, atrocious and cowardly description."

The following September the first victims of Illinois lawlessness began coming to St. Louis. On September 15 the *Weekly Reveille* reported that "many Mormons have visited St. Louis during the week for the purchase of provisions. They state that there is a general combination of Illinois and Missouri people against them. Provisions on their way to Nauvoo are in every case intercepted and the friendly farmers ill treated. The design is to starve them out of the country." Also during that same September what was perhaps the first Mormon conference ever held in St. Louis took place on the 29th. The president of the branch at that time was James Riley, and the main purpose of the conference was to sustain the Council of the Twelve in Nauvoo.

There was a second conference that year, on November 10. Orson Hyde was present at this time, along with 233 others – "the largest congregation ever assembled in this city to hear an Elder of the Latter-day Saints preach," reported the *Times and Seasons*. Among other things, Elder Hyde encouraged the Saints to subscribe to the official Mormon newspaper, the *Times and Seasons*, published in Nauvoo, and called upon all Mormons in the area to unite with the branch.

The branch continued to grow and prosper. In January 1845 Orson Hyde returned and delivered a lecture on Mormonism and things in general at their headquarters next door to the Liberty Engine House. Upon his return to Nauvoo he reported in the *Times and Seasons* that: I was highly pleased with the spirit that prevails among the Saints in that place. They are united in fellowship – they are one in heart, one in faith, and one in their resolutions to serve and honor the Lord, to uphold the regular authorities of the Church, and listen to the counsel and instruction of the Quorum of the Twelve.

Another conference was held on February 10 in the Franklin Hall and 403 (329 members, 4 High Priests, 18 Seventies, 25 Elders, 15 Priests, 6 Teachers, and 6 Deacons) were present – nearly double the congregation of the preceding November conference. This conference considered and resolved many things, including the resolve to sustain the Quorum of the Twelve, to help rear and finish the temple, and to patronize the *Times and Seasons* (such things as would hold the group together and strengthen its union with Nauvoo). The conference also resolved that "We view with mingled emotions of grief and surprise, the proceedings of the highest court in the State of Illinois, in taking away the chartered rights of Nauvoo." They also resolved that "although surrounded by apostates... we feel perfectly safe in the midst of an enlightened people, who alike know how to appreciate political liberty and religious freedom; and who have too much respect for the sanctity of constitutional rights, to trample upon the law and the rights of others."

On January 9, 1846 the *St. Louis Organ* commented on the persecution of Mormons in Illinois. After criticizing Governor Ford for having acted unwisely, the paper said, "It is notorious that the great 'Mormon Eaters' of the upper Missouri were the greatest scamps in the country, and we have very good reason to believe that the same remarks would apply to the tribe who are now persecuting them in Illinois." The *Organ* then quoted the *Peoria Register* to the effect that Joseph and Hyrum had been murdered in "cold blood... an act of atrocity unparalleled in the history of the age," and that the persecutors will "continue to have apologists for their misdeeds, in the shape of some sixpenny journal of the calibre of the Warsaw Signal, Quincy Whig & Co."

The exodus from Nauvoo commenced in February and continued throughout the year. That July, when Brigham Young was preparing to winter in the Council Bluffs, Iowa area, he instructed the Church trustees in Nauvoo to determine the number of Saints in St. Louis who wanted to join him. Apparently not many were ready or able to go at that time, for there is no mention of the St. Louis Saints moving to Winter Quarters. (In August, Bishop Newel K. Whitney came to St. Louis from Winter Quarters to purchase sixty tons of supplies, and it is possible that some of the Saints from St. Louis returned to the Winter Quarters area with him.)

We do know, however, that many Mormons from Illinois who did not go west with Brigham Young did come to St. Louis – especially during the "Mormon

War" in Nauvoo of September 10-13 when mobs drove the remaining Mormons out. The *St. Louis Daily Union* of September 22, for example, reported that "The New Haven brought a number of families from Nauvoo to St. Louis. Many Mormons are leaving Nauvoo." On September 29 the same paper said, "The New Haven brought down from Keokuk some forty families of Mormons whose purpose it is to settle in this city." Many of these Saints settled in St. Louis, but others stayed only long enough to get an "outfit" in order to join Brigham Young.

That same September the Church trustees in Nauvoo came to St. Louis to collect funds and goods to relieve the distress of the exiles. In reference to this, the *St. Louis Union* of October 5 printed the following: "MORMON SUFFERERS IN NAUVOO: The public has been apprised that Mr. Heywood is here as a committee to receive contributions of food, clothing, or anything else that the benevolent may choose to send to the sufferers."

A week later the *St. Louis Weekly Reveille* published a lengthy announcement from Peter G. Camden, Mayor of St. Louis. "THE MORMON SUFFERS: In the recent expulsion and flight of the Mormons from Nauvoo and its vicinity, many of the poorest, most friendless and helpless have been left behind... How or why these unfortunates are in their present condition, there is no time now to inquire... it should suffice that we have the highest authority and encouragement for believing it is always 'more blessed to give than to receive'... it is hoped that the people of St. Louis will, on this occasion, maintain their former high character for sympathy and liberality."

In October, Brigham Young sent word to Joseph A. Stratton, who had succeeded Riley as branch president, to send as many men west as possible with the understanding that they could bring their families later. Again the sources are silent regarding how many, if any, left St. Louis at that time. We do know, however, that in spite of all these difficulties, the well-known Mormon penchant for making the best of things brought about in October the organization of the St. Louis Lyceum, devoted to adult education and the study of the gospel.

The new year of 1847 started out with a conference on January 31 at which time it was reported that in the St. Louis area there were 1,478 members present. Since prior to the exodus from Nauvoo, there had only been about 400 members in St. Louis, many Mormons must have come to St. Louis from Illinois, and most of the 1846 migrants must have decided to remain in St. Louis rather than push on to troubled Nauvoo or distant Winter Quarters.

The branch also got a new president. After President Stratton left for Winter Quarters in February, Nathaniel H. Felt was called to succeed him. In Winter Quarters Elder Stratton reported two cases of polygamy in St. Louis to President Young who prudently sent word back that the two polygamists should join the main body of Saints as quickly as possible to avoid trouble in St. Louis.

Since there were already more than 1,500 Saints in St. Louis, and other hundreds on the way from Europe, and since President Young had not yet settled his people anywhere, St. Louis was officially designated as "a gathering place for the driven from Nauvoo and the converted from Europe coming up from New Orleans," and the branch organization was expanded to that of a district.

THE DISTRICT, 1847-1854
To enable the local leaders to fulfill their new responsibilities as a "gathering" and outfitting place, the original branch was divided into six branches on March 25, each with its own presidency (but all using the same place of worship), and became therefore a "conference" or district – the only one in the Church for sometime outside of wherever Brigham Young happened to be, and Felt became the district president. During the rest of that year three new branches (Gravois, Dry Hill, Missouri, and Alton, Illinois) were organized, some Saints were shipped to Winter Quarters, hundreds more were received from Europe, and money and teams were sent to help with the forthcoming move from Winter Quarters.

So many hundred emigrants flooded into the city that President Felt took most of the Mound House Hotel for temporary housing, and rented the larger and more suitable Concert Hall on Market Street (between Second and Third Streets, west side) for Sunday services. He divided the Gravois branch into four units, one of which was Welsh, and found himself by September 1849 shepherding from 3,000 to 4,000 members -- the largest district in the Church. (The population of St. Louis was then about 65,000.)

Even throughout the great cholera epidemic and fire of 1849 the district continued to grow. The *Frontier Guardian* reported on June 13 that "great accessions are made to the Church in St. Louis in the midst of fire, cholera, and death."

We learn something of the affairs of the district from John Taylor who spent some time in the city that winter while en route to a mission in France. He wrote his family: After a long absence I now sit down to write you. I have been in this city about three weeks... Here the Saints have a magnificent hall and a splendid band and do things up in good style.

Emigrants continued to come in. On June 17 the *Frontier Guardian* noted that "During the past three or four days not less than 1,000 emigrants... passed through St. Louis on their way to the Great Salt Lake." The St. Louis press took careful note of the arrival of the emigrants and their activities. On May 8, 1851, for example, the *Missouri Republican* carried the following: Although we have no Mormon Church in St. Louis, and though these people have no other class or permanent interest in our city, yet their numerical strength here is greater than may be imagined. Our city is the greatest recruiting point for Mormon emigrants from England and the Eastern States.

There are at this time in St. Louis about three thousand English Mormons, nearly all of whom are masters of some trade, or have acquired experience in some profession, which they follow now. As we said, they have no Church, but they attend divine services twice each Sunday at Concert Hall, and they perform their devotional duties with the same regularity, if not in the same style as their brethren in the valley.

We hear frequently of Mormon balls and parties, and Concert Hall on several occasions filled with persons gathered to witness Mormon theatrical performances. We have witnessed the congregation as it issued from the hall and at religious meetings on Sunday, and certainly we think it does not compare unfavorably with other congregations.

On June 28 the same paper reported that "upwards of 1,000 had arrived at St. Louis since spring, not more than 600 of whom had been able to leave."

Despite heroic efforts to ship the emigrants west (more than eleven companies left in 1852), the district continued to grow. In October of that year, Horace S. Eldridge was sent from Utah to preside over the district and to act as General Emigration Agent for the Church in St. Louis. Even though during the 1853 and 1854 seasons he purchased about 800 wagons and 4,000 head of cattle to ship emigrants with, the district flourished.

Finally at the 1854 April Conference the leaders in Salt Lake City designated St. Louis as a place to "which the Latter-day Saints might gather with approbation who were unable to go directly through to Utah" and appointed Erastus Snow of the Quorum of the Twelve to go to St. Louis and organize a stake, direct emigration, and preside generally over the whole Church in the area. At the same time Milo Andrus was called to preside over the stake which Elder Snow was to organize.

THE STAKE

Elder Andrus left Salt Lake City more than two months before Elder Snow and on May 30 arrived in St. Louis where he was met by Orson Pratt and Horace S. Eldridge. On August 28, Elder Snow arrived in St. Louis and boarded with Elder Andrus. A few days later, on September 12, he wrote to Franklin D. Richards in England that: Brother Andrus had succeeded well in his labors here and on my arrival he was stirring up the Saints to renew their covenants in baptism and nearly all have done so... after this month we shall leave Concert Hall and occupy (lease) the Old Methodist Church on Fourth Street and a spacious building with a gallery, which will be under our entire control, including a basement with three rooms, suitable for councils, storage, or rendezvous for our emigration... I propose calling a special General Conference in this place on the first Saturday and Sunday in November.

On the following November 4, the most important single event in history of the Church in early St. Louis took place – the organization of the first St. Louis Stake by Elder Snow – the sixteenth stake to be organized in the Church. Milo Andrus was sustained as president, with Charles Edwards and George Gardner as counselors; a High Council of twelve men was also organized. The stake consisted of at least fifteen branches in Missouri, Illinois, and Iowa, and 1,320 members attended from the following branches: St. Louis First, 59; St. Louis Second and Third, 164; St. Louis Fourth, 157; St. Louis Fifth, 158; St. Louis Sixth, 250; Gravois, 216; Dry Hill, 45; Bellefontaine, 23; Alton, Illinois, 102; Centerville, Illinois, 8; Keokuk, Iowa, 35; Bluff City, Iowa, 71; Maquoketa, Iowa, 16; and Fairfield, Iowa, 16.

That same month Elder Snow established the *St. Louis Luminary*, a weekly newspaper, to promote "science, religion, general intelligence, and news of the day." He used a basement room in the chapel for an office. The first issue appeared November 22 and for a year, until December 18, 1855, it advocated and defended the Restored Gospel.

As with the district, the biggest work of the stake was emigration. Indeed the sketchy records of that time reveal little else, and the arrival and departure of emigrants is faithfully chronicled. Many were shipped as far west as possible on the Missouri River, and others overland by wagon and team.

In spite of the hundreds who left for Utah, the stake continued to grow. At the April 1855 conference, 1,661 members were present, all but 140 of whom were in the St. Louis area. The records of the October conference that year show a membership of 2,044 in thirty branches in Missouri, Illinois, Iowa, Indiana, Ohio and Kansas Territory. That fall both Andrus and Snow returned to Utah, and the senior member of the High Council, James Henry Hart became the next stake president on October 6.

On January 7, 1857, Elder Snow instituted the "Reformation," a reform movement which had commenced in Utah in mid-1856 and swept throughout the Church in 1856 and 1857 until every Saint was rededicated to the Kingdom through baptism or purged from membership. Snow visited all the wards and branches in the area, preaching, excommunication, and re-baptizing. In February, Apostles Parley P. Pratt and George A. Smith were sent to St. Louis to help with the Reformation.

The great Reformation proved to have been the last major activity of the organized St. Louis Stake. The threatening "Utah War" of 1857 pretty much killed it. To strengthen the Church's defense against the U.S. Army advancing on Utah, Brigham Young called Erastus Snow and all others who could leave St. Louis that summer. This, essentially, brought an end of the stake. The razing of the chapel later that year by its owner was the symbolic end. Among those who left was James H. Hart, the second president of the stake. Thereafter the sources regarding the Church in St. Louis are even more scanty than for the earlier period.

THE INTER-STAKE PERIOD, 1858-1958
A CENTURY-LONG WAIT

Apparently Brother Eldridge more or less presided over the Saints in St. Louis until he returned to Utah in 1858. The Dry Hill branch kept records until April 14, 1859, but they are mainly a record of those who emigrated. Erastus Snow passed through St. Louis during November 1860 en route east on a mission.

There is reference to an Elder Elijah Thomas working here in 1861. From 1862 to 1868 and again from 1870 to 1877, St. Louis was a branch of the Indian Territory Mission. The branch had 75 members in 1864. Thereafter, St. Louis was part of the Southwestern States Mission until 1904.

In June 1877, a conference was held in the Broadway Hall at 1310 N Broadway with 42 in attendance. Thereafter there was very little Mormon activity until 1896. A few families met in each other's home to keep the spark alive. One special event was a concert by the Mormon Tabernacle Choir September 2, 1893 in the Music Hall of the Exposition Building.

In 1896, Salt Lake City sent two elders, Melvin J. Ballard, a future apostle, and Ezra Christensen, to reorganize the St. Louis branch and to renew Church activities in the area. The branch took root and members met in each other's homes. By 1903, the missionaries were able to turn the direction of the branch over to a local member. Theodore J. Martin, who remained the leader for seventeen years.

In 1904, Utah had an exhibit at the St. Louis World's Fair which cheered the local membership and in that same year the branch became part of the East Missouri District of the Central States Mission. In 1906 a formal MIA was organized and a Relief Society in 1907.

From 1906 to 1916, the Saints rented the so-called Assembly Hall at 4265 Easton Avenue and used it for religious services. Previously it had been Reinhart's Meat Market. It was at this time, in 1915, that a young missionary named Spencer W. Kimball was called to St. Louis to become District President.

For years the branch worked to obtain a more suitable building for their Church activities and one of the last duties of District President Kimball was to arrange, for $6,500, to purchase an old chapel from the Reformed Dutch Church of America located at 5195 Maple Avenue. On September 3, 1916 the Saints finally held their first meeting in their new quarters. On November 26, James E. Talmage of the Quorum of the Twelve Apostles dedicated this chapel. Here the branch remained for many years.

In 1920 James C. Brinkerhoff succeeded Brother Martin as branch president. Ten years later, in 1930, the branch had grown to 402 members and in 1932 was divided into the South Saint Louis Branch and the Maple Avenue Branch, but this was not successful and in 1938 the two were rejoined as the St. Louis Branch with Roy D. Hoppie as president. Then came World War II and the branch marked time, not growing much.

RAPID GROWTH FOLLOWING WORLD WAR II

In 1945 the period of slow development ended for good. Roy W. Oscarson and family moved to St. Louis. Brother Oscarson arrived from San Francisco to the home office of Edison Brothers Shoe Company, Inc., eventually rising to become Senior Vice President and a member of the Board of Directors. That same year Brother Hoppie moved to Texas and on October 28, Roy Oscarson succeeded him as branch president.

Under President Oscarson's dynamic leadership, the Saints soon outgrew their Maple Avenue chapel and were urged to build a more suitable edifice for themselves. A building fund was commenced, the old chapel was sold in 1947, and for two years the Saints met in various temporary quarters, including the Hamilton School.

Then in 1949 one of the most important events of recent Mormon history in St. Louis took place. On September 4, 1949 George Albert Smith, President of the Church, dedicated the new chapel at 4720 Jamieson, the first chapel the Mormons had ever built in the area. At that time the chapel was considered to be the finest LDS edifice between Salt Lake City and the nation's capitol.

On this dedicatory occasion Francis W. Brown, President of the Central States Mission, turned the direction of the East Missouri District from the missionaries over to the local Saints, and Roy Oscarson became president of the district (as well as of the branch), choosing Dudly Brown as a counselor. The district then had nine branches in St. Louis, Hannibal, Columbia, Mexico, Jefferson City, Rolla, and Kirksville, Missouri, and in nearby East St. Louis and Belleville, Illinois. (Shortly afterwards Dr. Paul Keller succeeded Brother Oscarson as president of the St. Louis Branch.)

During the fall of 1951 a recent member of the Quorum of the Twelve, Spencer W. Kimball toured the East Missouri District, visiting St. Louis. Three years later, in 1954, the St. Louis Branch was again divided, this time successfully, along Clayton Road into the North and South Branches.

ROY W. OSCARSON, 1958-1969

Once the momentum of growth and success was started, it increased rapidly. Only four years later, in 1958, as a result of President Oscarson's leadership and the encouragement of Alvin R. Dyer, President of the Central States Mission (1954-58), the East Missouri District became the second St. Louis Stake. On June 1, 1958, two members of the Quorum of the Twelve, Harold B. Lee (later President), and Mark E. Peterson, organized the 265th Stake in Zion. District President Oscarson became the President of the new Stake, selecting as his counselors Henry Beal and Clifford Stutz.

At that time five distant branches were turned back to the mission and the new, more compact stake consisted of the following six wards and branches: St. Louis First Ward, 565 members; St. Louis Second Ward, 455 members; Rolla Branch, 107 members; Belleville Ward, 159 members; East St. Louis Ward, 555 members; and the Alton Ward, 121 members; for a total of 1,738 members, of which 649 were present for the creation of the Stake. The first General Authority assigned to visit the new St. Louis Stake for its Stake Conference was Elder Spencer W. Kimball in October 1958.

Thereafter the new stake grew rapidly. Many Mormons from the west settled in the St. Louis Stake for business and professional reasons; many came to the fine universities, medical, and dental schools; still others came to the large military installations – Scott Air Force Base in Illinois and Fort Leonard Wood in Missouri.

During the eleven-year administration of President Oscarson (1958-1969) the stake grew by eight units. The St. Louis Third Ward was formed in May 1961 (in 1963 the Belleville and East St. Louis wards merged, and in 1964 the new Fairview Heights Ward was created from these two older wards), the Union Branch in 1963, the Litchfield, Illinois Branch during January 1965, the St. Charles, Missouri Branch in February 1966, the St. Louis Fourth Ward in September 1966, the Ft. Leonard Wood, Missouri Branch in March 1967, the St. Louis Fifth Ward in February 1968, the De Soto, Missouri (now Hillsboro) Branch in October 1968 with a total stake membership of 4,530 as of September 31, 1969.

As already noted, when President Oscarson became Stake President in 1958 there were 1,758 members. Under his leadership the Stake grew by 2,792 members for a remarkable growth of 261 percent. Furthermore, four chapels were built and dedicated (St. Louis Second Ward, St. Louis Third Ward and Stake Center, Alton Ward, and Fairview Ward), and four other pieces of property were bought in Baldwin, Hillsboro, St. Charles, and on Butler Hill Road. One of President Oscarson's main teachings was, "Let us get the Saints properly housed that they may have a full Church Program and show the gospel off to advantage."

In 1958, the Mormon Tabernacle Choir sang in Kiel Auditorium, in 1959 the BYU Delta Phi Chorus gave a concert, and in 1966 the BYU Acappella Chorus performed in the Stake. Since 1959, General Priesthood meetings have been brought into the St. Louis Stake Center by a closed-wire broadcast. Other sessions of the General Conference have been on television since 1966, and beginning in 1967 the St. Louis Stake became headquarters for all regional and area meetings. In passing it might also be noted that Alvah D. Boggs, grandson of Governor Lilburn W. Boggs who issued the Mormon Extermination Order in 1858 joined the Church in St. Louis in 1958.

On September 19, 1969, Roy W. Oscarson was called to be Regional Representative of the Council of the Twelve, and was released as President of the St. Louis Stake. He served with his usual distinction in this calling until 1976 when he was called to preside over the Scotland, Edinburgh Mission. When President Oscarson arrived in Scotland he became the third member of his family then serving as a European mission president. One son, Grant Richard Oscarson, was President of the Swedish Stockholm Mission, and another son, Paul Rent Oscarson, was President of the Swedish Goteberg Mission.

BOYD F. SCHENK, 1969-1974

The next president of the St. Louis Stake was Boyd F. Schenk who came to St. Louis from California in 1958 to eventually become President of Pet, Inc. Prior to 1968, Brother Schenk had served on the St. Louis Stake High Council (1958-1959), as Bishop of St. Louis First Ward (1959-61), and as Bishop of the new St. Louis Third Ward (1961-69). He chose Richard Grant Rees and Walter W. Wiest as counselors in the Stake Presidency. President Schenk liked to tell the Saints, "The secret of a happy life is to have a great time living righteously."

Under President Schenk the stake gained two units and lost two. During January 1970, the Farmington, Missouri Branch was added to the St. Louis stake from the North Central States Mission, and in September 1970, the Fairview Second Ward was created in Illinois. The two units lost were in April 1970 when Elder Spencer W. Kimball created the new Columbia, Missouri Stake, which acquired the Rolla Ward, and the Fort Leonard Wood Branch from the St. Louis Stake. This was the first of two times that the St. Louis Stake had been divided. Land for the Litchfield chapel was also purchased, a chapel in Union was acquired, and in 1974 the Farmington chapel was dedicated.

Other important developments under President Schenk's administration include the creation of a Stake Building Fund into which all units pay and from which all may draw, the organization of an Institute of Religion which began with one instructor in 1972, the creation of a Branch Genealogical Library in 1971, and the inauguration of the annual BYU Education Week Program in 1974.

During April 1974, Bishop R. Don Oscarson of the Second Ward presented the premier of his music-drama, City of Joseph. Later this production was taken to Nauvoo, Illinois and shown to an audience including Spencer W. Kimball of the Quorum of the Twelve. City of Joseph has become a major annual production at Nauvoo, attracting as many as 40,000 during its run of five nights each August. In 1976, City of Joseph was an official National, State, and Church Bicentennial event.

During June 1974, as President Roy W. Oscarson before him, President Schenk was called to be a Regional Representative of the Council of the Twelve. At that time stake membership was 4,900, an increase of about 400 members, in spite of the stake being divided. President Schenk served as a Regional Representative until 1976.

RICHARD GRANT REES, JUNE 1974-PRESENT

Born in Croydon, Utah, educated at Utah State University, Richard Grant Rees served for four years in World War II as a Marine pilot in the South Pacific. President Rees came to St. Louis from Chicago eventually to become Vice-President of Operations at Ozark Air Lines, Inc. Prior to 1974 Brother Rees served in the St. Louis Stake as a District Councilman (1957-58), as Bishop of the St. Louis Second Ward (1958-69), and as First Counselor to President Schenk (1969-74). He chose Sherman L. Hislop and R. Don Oscarson as counselors in the Stake Presidency. Stake membership as of June 1974 was 5,159. President Rees is well known for his teaching, "Brethren, improve your home teaching and all else in your wards and branches will also improve."

During his four-year administration (to 1978) the St. Louis Stake gained three units and lost five. In 1975, a branch in Edwardsville, Illinois and the St. Louis Sixth Ward were created; in 1976, the St. Louis Seventh Ward was brought into existence. The five units lost were on March 14, 1976 when the new Fairview Heights Illinois Stake was created by Elder Gordon B. Hinkley. This was the second time the St. Louis Stake had been divided. In addition, the stake lost the Fairview Ward, Fairview Second Ward, Alton Ward, and the Litchfield and Edwardsville Branches, all to the Illinois. At the time of the division the St. Louis Stake had grown from 1,758 members in 1958 to 5,229, for an increase of 3,489 members, or a growth of 300 percent. The reduced St. Louis Stake then consisted of eleven units and 3,785 members.

Even after this division, President Rees continued to hold two sessions of Stake Conference, one session for each half of the stake. The positive result was that 45 percent of stake membership attended, compared with a proceeding average of about 27 percent. Membership as of May 1, 1978 was 4,574, an increase of 589, or a growth of 15 percent in two years.

Other important events during President Rees' administration as of July, 1978, include his dedication of the first, second, and third phases of the St. Charles Chapel, phase two of the Farmington Chapel, and phase one of the Hillsboro Chapel. Furthermore the Litchfield Chapel was completed just before the stake was divided. A group of 100 members of the St. Louis Stake flew by charter flight to attend the 1974 dedication of the Washington, DC Temple by President Spencer W. Kimball. In 1977, a new mission was created with headquarters in St. Louis – the Missouri St. Louis Mission. President Rees was also the first Stake President in St. Louis empowered to dedicate chapels and ordain Seventies and Bishops.

In 1974 and 1976 President R. Don Oscarson and Dr. Stanley B. Kimball, acting for the Mormon Pioneer Trail Foundation, placed two markers in St. Louis. The first was on the outside wall of the Missouri Athletic Club at 4th St. and Washington Ave., and marks the site of the first building used as an LDS chapel in St. Louis, 1854-57. The second is a gravestone in Bellefontaine Cemetery in remembrance of the infant daughter, Emily, of President James H. Hart who died in 1854. This gravestone also honors all others of Emily's faith who died in early St. Louis.

PRESIDENT SPENCER W. KIMBALL AND ST. LOUIS: 1915-1978 MISSIONARY-APOSTLE-PROPHET

Coming from Thatcher, Arizona, originally called to the Swiss-German Mission, Elder Spencer W. Kimball, because of the outbreak of World War I, was sent to the Central States Mission during the fall of 1914. His Mission President, Samuel O. Bennion, impressed with the twenty-year-old elder, soon called him in 1915 to St. Louis to become President of the East Missouri Conference (District) and to take charge of twenty-five other missionaries all older than himself.

Determined to make good, the young elder tracted all over the city and held regular street meetings on North Market Street near Union Station in order to invite people to their humble rented hall at 4265 Easton Avenue. When opportunity came he would play the piano to entertain, improve meetings, or to interest people in his message. Once, when tracting, he noticed a Kimball Piano and asked the lady at the door if he might play a hymn on it. He often wondered what sort of an impression he made on her.

There was time for fun too. The missionaries enjoyed visiting the Chain of Rocks Park above the Mississippi River and plenty of ice cream cones, an invention of the St. Louis World's Fair of 1904.

Elder Kimball and companions first roomed with a Sister Titlow near the Easton Hall and later had a room with Mrs. Mary Frank, not then a member, across the street from the hall. One of his last duties was to arrange for the purchase of the Maple Avenue chapel. Finally, Elder Kimball was released and arrived back home New Year's Day, 1917.

Elder Kimball eventually became a member of the Quorum of the Twelve in 1949 and eight years later in 1951, finally received an assignment to tour the Central States Mission, an assignment which returned him to St. Louis after thirty-five years.

It now appears providential that after the organization of the second St. Louis Stake on June 1, 1958, that Elder Kimball would be the first General Authority sent to preside at the first St. Louis Stake Conference, October 4, 1958.

Elder Kimball returned to St. Louis again in 1961, conducting a special missionary meeting. He was indirectly connected with the St. Louis Stake in April 1970, when he created the Columbia Missouri Stake taking away two of the stake's units, the Rolla Ward and the Ft. Leonard Wood Branch.

Perhaps the single most important event to transpire (prior to today, July 2, 1978) in this and the earlier St. Louis Stake was on February 5, 1977 when Elder Kimball, by then President since December 30, 1973, and his counselors, N. Eldon Tanner, and Marion G. Romney, Elder Gordon B. Hinkley of the Council of the Twelve, and James A. Cullimore of the First Council of Seventy, conducted a Solemn Assembly in the St. Louis Stake Center for eleven stakes and two missions – something a President of the Church hadn't ever been able to do in his former mission field.

In March, 1980, the St. Louis Missouri South Stake was created, and Verner L. Stromberg was called as stake president. Additionally, during this time, welfare farms were purchased, and the regional bishop's storehouse was built, and later dedicated on March 16, 1985. The St. Louis Missouri Stake was reorganized on March 20, 1983, with Allen Christiansen called as stake president. David B. Haight presided over this reorganization, and dedicated the new stake center in Chesterfield during this time.

three • SAINT LOUIS MISSION HISTORY

The Missouri St. Louis Mission was organized in 1976 with Norman W. Olsen called to preside. It was created out of the Missouri Independence Mission which had it roots in what was originally called the Indian Territory Mission which was organized in April of 1883, and presided over by the Apostle George Teasdale.

Andrew Kimball, father of President Spencer W. Kimball, presided from January 1885 to April 1887. The name of the mission was changed to Southwestern States Mission in March of 1898, with William T. Jack presiding. In April of 1904 the name was changed to Central States Mission with James G. Duffin presiding. Succeeding mission presidents included Samuel O. Bennion, Elias W. Woodruff, John F. Bowman, Thomas C. Romney, Francis W. Brown, Orville J. Ellsworth, Alvin R. Dyer, Samuel R. Carpenter, G. Carlos Smithe, Jr., Wayne Player, James B. Keysor and Brian F. West.

In August of 1969, the South Central States Mission was organized having been split off from the Central States Mission with Brian F. West presiding. In June of 1970, the mission was changed to Kansas Missouri Mission. J. Stuart McMaster and Graham W. Doxey presided while the mission held this name. In 1974, the name changed to the Missouri Independence Mission while Graham W. Doxey presided. Those who followed him have included: Edward A. Johnson, Lawrence Read Flake, Richard Bartford, Lloyd J. Cope, Michael H. Holmes, Thomas Murray and Ben E. Rawlings.

The beginnings of missionary work in what has been the foregoing missions occurred in 1830 and 1831, six months after the organization of the Church on April 6, 1830, when Oliver Cowdery, Parley P. Pratt, Peter Whitmore, Jr., and Richard Ziba Peterson were called by special revelation (D&C 32) on a mission to preach to the Lamanites. They arrived in Independence, Missouri, in the early part of 1831. Soon after they crossed the border into that part of the country now included in the state of Kansas, then designated as Indian Territory. They opened up a mission among the Delaware Indians. The mission prospered but the Indian agent compelled the missionaries to cease their labors among the natives, thus ending the first Indian Mission of the Church.

MISSOURI ST. LOUIS MISSION PRESIDENTS

The following mission presidents have served since the organization of the Missouri St. Louis Mission: President Norman W. Olsen 1976-1980, President Leon Hartshorn 1980-1983, President Charles Tate 1983-1986, President Donald Rydalch 1986-1989, President John Frame 1989-1992, President Wayne McGrath 1992-1995, President Stuart Preece 1995-1998.

four • **TEMPLE DISTRICT STAKE HISTORIES**

The St. Louis Temple District includes a total of 33 stakes within Missouri and the surrounding states of Illinois, Indiana, Kansas, Kentucky, and Tennessee. Following are brief histories of these stakes, in alphabetical order, and biographies of their current stake presidents. Twenty-five of the thirty-three stakes are included, while eight stakes weren't able to respond: Cape Girardeau, Missouri; Joplin, Missouri; Lexington, Kentucky; Memphis, Tennessee; Owingsville, Kentucky; Papillion, Nebraska; Platte City, Missouri and Springfield, Illinois.

ST. LOUIS MISSOURI TEMPLE DISTRICT

BLOOMINGTON INDIANA	President Bruce Bennett Hronek
CAPE GIRARDEAU MISSOURI	President William J. Burke
CHAMPAIGN ILLINOIS	President Joseph Shldi
COLUMBIA MISSOURI	President John C. Jorgensen
EVANSVILLE INDIANA	President James Wayne Hansen
HOPKINSVILLE KENTUCKY	President Michael Richardson
INDEPENDENCE MISSOURI	President C. Kent Wood
JOPLIN MISSOURI	President David L. Tillman
KANSAS CITY MISSOURI	President Gordon D. Goodman
LENEXA KANSAS	President Donald D. Dashler
LEXINGTON KENTUCKY	President L. Paul Moeck
LIBERTY MISSOURI	President Michael Wiley Barker
LINCOLN NEBRASKA	President Maury Wintle Schooff
LOUISVILLE KENTUCKY	President William Price Norton
MEMPHIS TENNESSEE	President Donald B. Spene
MEMPHIS TENNESSEE NORTH	President Calvin K. Hansen
NAUVOO ILLINOIS	President Durell Noland Nelson
NEW ALBANY INDIANA	President John Ray Crawford
O'FALLON ILLINOIS	President Donald McCain
OLATHE KANSAS	President Nathan Y. Jarvis
OMAHA NEBRASKA	President Arthur H. Taylor
OWINGSVLLLE KENTUCKY	President Gale K. Beaman
PADUCAH KENTUCKY	President Larry Watkins
PAPILLION NEBRASKA	President Evan Louis Butler
PLATTE CITY MISSOURI	President Ronald Stapled
SALINA KANSAS	President Thomas R. Coleman
SPRINGFIELD ILLINOIS	President Alonzo J. Mackelprang
SPRINGFIELD MISSOURI	President Gerald Tim Goodman
SPRINGFIELD MISSOURI SOUTH	President Stanfey Petersen
ST. LOUIS MISSOURI	President Grant Richard Oscarson
ST. LOUIS MISSOURI NORTH	President H. Kent Pviunson
ST. LOUIS MISSOURI SOUTH	President George Dee Bankhead
TOPEKA KANSAS	President Dennis H. Karpowitz

Long before Indiana had its first stake, the Prophet Joseph Smith led Zions Camp through Indianapolis and into Illinois near Terry Haute. Some members still remember their parents reminiscing about the days when the only formal Church services were held by missionaries who passed through three or four times a year. Eventually, branches were organized, meeting in rented halls. A building was erected in what is now Linton Ward and the site is still called the "Mormon Temple."

The full Church program for most units came with organization of the Indianapolis Stake in 1959. It was divided to form the Bloomington Stake in 1979 with Hollis R. Johson as president. Many of its branches have since become wards.

BRUCH BENNETT HRONEK was set apart as stake president on February 15, 1996. A professor at Indiana State University, he is a former stake executive secretary, high council member, seminary teacher, institute instructor, stake mission president, stake young men's president, branch president, bishop and high priest group leader. He was born and reared in Pocatello, Idaho. He is married to Sylvia Smith and they have five children.

The Church's history in this area dates to early Nauvoo days, but its return was slow following the exodus of the Saints to the west starting in 1846. Members began to appear, one family at a time, in the early 1900s. In the 1920s, home Sunday Schools were authorized. Later, members traveled many miles to attend meetings at branches at Farmer City and Chanute Air Force Base at Rantoul.

The Champaign-Urbana Branch was formed in 1941. Its members met in the Champaign City Council chamber.

Other branches were formed later, and mission districts grew, increased in membership and divided. The first area chapel was dedicated in 1954 by Elder Hugh B. Brown, then an assistant to the Twelve. The Illinois Stake, as it was then called, was formed in 1963 with Ross A. Kelly as president. There have been many reorganizations and boundary changes.

JOSEPH WILLIAM STUCKI was set apart as stake president on Dec 5, 1993. A professor at the University of Illinois, he is a former bishop and served a mission in Brazil. He has traveled extensively professionally and has published about 70 scientific articles. He was born and reared in Rexburg, Idaho. He is married to Penny Jo Nickel and they have six children.

COLUMBIA MISSOURI STAKE

Church membership has grown steadily since much of the stake's current territory was organized in 1953 as the Northeast Missouri District of the Central States Mission. Units were started in many communities. Some prospered; other did not survive.

The Columbia Stake was organized on April 19, 1970 by Elder Spencer W. Kimball, then of the Council of the Twelve Apostles, with Sam Richards as stake president. New units at Rolla, Fort Leonard Wood and Camdenton were added. Stake offices were originally housed in Columbia meetinghouse on Business Route 63. A new stake center was dedicated in April 1996.

JOHN CHRISTIAN JORGENSEN was set apart as stake president November 1991. He has been a business executive for the past 25 years in Moberly, Missouri. Born and reared in Salt Lake City, he is a former stake president's counselor, bishop's counselor, elders quorum president and branch president. He is married to Jacqueline Fae Plewe and they have five children.

EVANSVILLE INDIANA STAKE

Missionary activity in Indiana dates back to 1831, and Joseph Smith spent four weeks in Greenville, Indiana in 1832. In the early 1900s, missionaries and members faced strong opposition, sometimes even mob violence. The first meetings was held at the home of a nonmember family, Dr. and Mrs. McClaren at 600 Mulberry Street in Evansville. Later members bought and remodeled the former Bethany Christian Church at Edgar and Maryland Streets.

Formerly a district of the Indiana Indianapolis Mission, the Evansville Stake was organized on Oct. 19, 1975, by Elder Thomas S. Monson, then of the Council of Twelve Apostles, with Frank R. Fults Jr. as stake president. Its membership includes residents of Indiana, Kentucky and Illinois.

JAMES WAYNE HANSEN was set apart as stake president in October 1988. He is a research physician for Mead Johnson & Co., a subsidiary of the Bristol-Myers Corp., and is on the medical staff at Welborn Baptist Hospital. He is a former stake president's counselor, bishop, high council member and bishop's counselor. He was born and reared in California. He is married to Karen Lyon and they have nine children.

HOPKINSVILLE KENTUCKY STAKE

The area's Latter-day Saint history dates to the 1830s when Wilford Woodruff walked from town to town as a missionary. The first branch president, George Addison, and his family grew tobacco as a fundraiser for the first chapel in Elkton, Kentucky. Some of their descendants still serve as local Church leaders. Morgantown Branch became the first ward in Kentucky in 1971.

The Hopkinsville Stake was formed in 1978 with Robert L. Fears as stake president. A new stake center was built at 1118 Pin Oak Drive in 1985. In October 1996, six of the stake's units were taken to help form the Paducah Kentucky Stake.

MICHAEL A. RICHARDSON was set apart as stake president on October 9, 1993. A lawyer, he is a former bishop, high council member, stake clerk, stake mission president, stake young men president, bishop's counselor and scoutmaster. He was born and reared in Hopkinsville. He and his wife, Patricia "Trish" Taylor, joined the Church in 1971. They have four children.

INDEPENDENCE MISSOURI STAKE

Church history abounds in the Independence area, which is mentioned frequently in the Doctrine & Covenants where it was designated as the "gathering place for the Saints." Members were expelled by mob violence in 1838-39 but a few decades later individual families were again settling in Jackson County.

The Church presence again became official in 1900 when the headquarters for the Southwestern States Mission was moved to Kansas City. Steady growth began after Independence became headquarters for the Central States Mission in 1907.

The Independence Stake was formed on March 25, 1971, by Elder Spencer W. Kimball, then acting president of the Council of the Twelve Apostles with Melvin James "Mick" Bennion as stake president. A new stake center was dedicated in 1978.

C. KENT WOOD was set apart as stake president on October 16, 1994. An employee of the U.S. Food and Drug Administration's criminal investigation office, he served 22 years in the Secret Service. He is a former stake president, bishop, high council member, elders quorum president and bishop's counselor. He was born in Columbia, Missouri. He is married to Carolyn Chapoton and they have three children.

KANSAS CITY MISSOURI STAKE

The return of Latter-day Saints to Jackson County began slowly after their expulsion in the 1830s, but the Kansas City Branch was organized in 1914 and by 1954 the area was a growing mission district and Kansas City was a mission headquarters as well.

The Kansas City Stake was organized on October 21, 1956, by Elders Harold B. Lee and Mark E. Peterson of the Quorum of the Twelve Apostles with Martin V. Whitbeck as the stake president. The stake was later divided to form the Independence Missouri Stake, then again to create the Olathe Kansas Stake and later to help form part of the Lenexa Kansas Stake. A new stake center at Blue Springs was occupied in August 1996.

GORDON D. GOODMAN was set apart as stake president of the Independence Missouri Stake December 1988, released in 1994 and called to preside over the Kansas City Stake. He is the owner of residential care facilities and has held many Church positions. He served a mission in Scotland. He is married to Leslie Christensen and they have five children.

LENEXA KANSAS STAKE

The Lenexa Stake was formed on October 16, 1994, at a conference of four stakes in the greater Kansas City area with Donald D. Deshler as stake president. It includes parts of Kansas and Missouri that are rich in Church history dating back to the early 1830s and 1840s, including Leavenworth.

A re-enactment of the mustering of the Mormon Battalion at Fort Leavenworth was conducted by members of the stake on August 3, 1996.

DONALD D. DESHLER was set apart as stake president when the Lenexa Stake was first organized in October 1994. Before that he had served as president of the Olathe Kansas Stake since 1989, and held many previous callings. He is a professor of special education and director of the Center for Research on Learning at the University of Kansas. He is married to Carol Ann Payne and they have four children.

LIBERTY MISSOURI STAKE

Steeped in Latter-Day Saint history dating back to the Prophet Joseph Smith's confinement in the Liberty Jail, the Liberty Stake was organized on Oct. 14, 1979, by Elder L. Tom Perry of the Quorum of the Twelve Apostles with Dell E. Johnson as stake president.

Three of the original stake's units helped form the new Lenexa Kansas Stake in 1994 and in March 1997 the Liberty Stake and Lenexa Stake were divided to form the new Platte City Stake.

MICHAEL WILEY BARKER was set apart as stake president on September 9 1990. A partner in a construction company in Kansas City, he is a former stake president's counselor, stake executive secretary, high council member, stake and ward young men president and ward clerk. He was born in Kansas City. He is married to Barbara Lee Sintzel and they have eight children.

LINCOLN NEBRASKA STAKE

James Hudson, a historian and later a state legislator, is the only Mormon on record who lived in the Lincoln area from 1846 to 1886, but a Latter-day Saint Sunday School was established in Lincoln in 1912 and by 1925 there were 125 members who met in an Odd Fellows hall. A meetinghouse was built in 1951.

The Lincoln Stake was formed in 1986 from what had previously been parts of the Omaha and Bellevue stakes, with Roy V. Sneddon as president. The Papillion Nebraska Stake was organized at the same time.

MAURY W. SCHOOF was set apart as stake president in April 1991. He is a retired educator and consultant. His previous Church callings include stake president's counselor, high council member, bishop, branch president, bishop's counselor, and seminary teacher. He was born in Ogden, Utah. He and his wife Margaret Joan Kennard Zitzman have three children.

LOUISVILLE KENTUCKY STAKE

Latter-day Saint history in the Louisville area began with tiny congregations established in smaller towns dating back to the 1890s. The Jonah Fork Branch was organized in late 1908 or early 1909 and the first Church building was dedicated there in 1910. The Louisville Branch was formed in 1930 and met above a saloon at Rosewood Avenue and Bardstown Ward.

The Louisville Stake was organized on January 17, 1971, with Henry H. Griffith as stake president. A new stake center was dedicated in January 1976 by Elder Ezra Taft Benson, then of the Quorum of the Twelve Apostles. By 1982 the stake had 19 units, some of which later became parts of the New Albany Indiana and Nashville Tennesee stakes.

WILLIAM P. NORTON was set apart as stake president in March 1990. A Church Education System employee for the past 26 years, he is currently coordinator for seminaries and institutes for the Kentucky and Indiana regions. He was born and reared in Preston, Idaho. He is married to Geraldine Bingham and they have seven children.

MEMPHIS TENNESSEE NORTH STAKE

Following a long period of "pioneering" by missionaries and members of small branches, the Memphis North Stake was organized on September 14, 1980, by Elder Gordon B. Hinckley, then of the Quorum of the Twelve Apostles, with Edward V. Martin as stake president.

Boundaries were realigned in 1988 and a new stake center was dedicated in February 1993. By 1996 the stake had about 3,100 members and by June 1997 it will have a full-time missionary in the field from each of its wards and branches.

CALVIN K. HANSEN was set apart as stake president on November 4, 1994. An actuarial consultant and former banking consultant, he is a former stake president's counselor, stake clerk, bishop's counselor, elders quorum president, high council member and scoutmaster. He is married to Lillian Beth Platt and they have five children.

NAUVOO ILLINOIS STAKE

Mormons first moved into the area now comprising Nauvoo Stake boundaries in large numbers during the winter of 1838-1839 to escape the persecution heaped upon them in Missouri. By the fall of 1839, many Church members had moved to an area known as Commerce (later to become Nauvoo), on October 5, 1839 during conference, Jospeh Smith Jr. asked "whether they wished to appoint this stake or not. Stating that he believed it to be a good place and suited for the Saints." It was unanimous in favor and William Marks became the stake president.

By the end of 1846 persecution had driven the Saints from the area and the Church from Illinois. For ninety years stake activity did not exist in Illinois until November 29, 1936 when a stake was organized in Chicago.

On February 18, 1979, President Ezra Taft Benson, then of the Quorum of the Twelve, organized the 1,000th stake of the Church, the Nauvoo Stake with Gene Lee Roymann being called as stake president

DURELL NELSON was set apart as stake president in 1993. He is employed as landscape architect for the Nauvoo Restoration Inc. He has served as ward and stake young men president, financial clerk, high council member and bishop. He is married to Kathy Randle and they are the parents of four children.

NEW ALBANY INDIANA STAKE

The East Central States Mission, Kentucky-Tennessee Mission and Kentucky Louisville Mission all played an intregal part in New Albany area Latter-day Saint history, as well as the Kentucky District, Kentucky Central District and Louisville Kentucky Stake.

The New Albany Stake was organized on October 24, 1982, in a division of the Louisville Stake by Elder David B. Haight and Elder James E. Faust, both of the Quorum of the Twelve Apostles, with Henry H. Griffeth as stake president. Although the stake stretches 150 miles from east to west and most unit are small, growth is continuing.

JOHN RAY CRAWFORD was set apart as stake president in November 1995. A chemical engineer, he has been a bishop, high council member, young mens president, seminary teacher and Sunday School president. He was born in Salem, Indiana and reared on a farm north of English, Indiana. He is married to Sherry Lee Coleman and they have three children.

O'FALLON ILLINOIS STAKE

Latter-day Saint history in this portion of Illinois situated across the Mississippi River from St. Louis was a gathering and outfitting center for the trek to the Salt Lake Valley. But in modern times, a branch was organized in East St. Louis in 1930. A branch was established in Belleville in 1949 and one in Alton in 1951. The area became a part of the St. Louis Stake when it was organized in 1958. The O'Fallon Stake was organized in 1976 by Elder Gordon B. Hinckley, then of the Council of the Twelve Apostles, with John O. Anderson as stake president. In October 1985 its four southernmost units were taken for the new Cape Girardeau Missouri Stake. A new stake center was dedicated in October 1993.

DONALD L. MCCAIN was set apart as stake president in October 1996. A businessman and entrepreneur, he is a former bishop, stake clerk, branch president, and bishop's counselor. He was born in Plantersville, Mississippi and reared in Mississippi and western Tennessee. He is married to Kerma Lee Pederson and they have four children.

OLATHE KANSAS STAKE

The Olathe Kansas Stake was created on October 19, 1986. It was the fourth stake formed in the Kansas City area. With Clifton D. Boyach being called as stake president.

Growth in the area continued until October 16, 1994 when the Olathe Kansas Stake and Kansas City Missouri Stake were both divided to form the new Lenexa Kansas Stake.

NATHAN YOUNG JARVIS was set apart as stake president in October 1994. By profession he is an illustrator and designer. He served a mission in Munich, Germany. Church callings have included bishop and counselor in the stake presidency. He is married to Michaela Maria Grunauer and they have five children.

OMAHA NEBRASKA STAKE

The temporary home of the Latter-day Saints at Winter Quarters in 1846, a gap of nearly 50 years ensued before Latter-day Saint resumed in eastern Nebraska. Small meetings were held in various places until the Omaha Branch was organized in 1915. In 1936 the pioneer statue by sculptor Avard Fairbanks was erected in Mormon Pioneer Cemetery and dedicated by President Heber J. Grant. In 1939 the Winter Quarters District was organized.

The Winter Quarters Stake was established in 1960 with Roy Cochran as president. In 1973 the name was changed to the Omaha Nebraska Stake. On April 18, 1997 a New Mormon Trail Center at historic Winter Quarters was dedicated by President Gordon B. Hinkley.

ARTHUR TAYLOR was set apart as stake president in 1996. A lawyer-businessman, he is vice president of administration for Coleman Powermate, a manufacturer of portable electric generators, pressure washers and air compressors. He was formerly president of the Kearney Nebraska Stake, held numerous other Church callings and served a mission in Ecuador. He is a native of Salt Lake City. He and his wife have eight children.

PADUCAH KENTUCKY STAKE

The Paducah Stake was organized on October 20, 1996, under the direction of Elder John Carmack of the Seventy, with Larry Wayne Watkins as stake president. The new stake was formed from potions of the Hopkinsville Kentucky and Evansville Indiana and Cape Girardeau Missouri stakes. It comprises four wards and four branches.

LARRY WAYNE WATKINS was set apart as stake president on October 20, 1996. He is president and CEO of Vision Enterprises, Business and Management Consultants. He was formerly president of Cape Girardeau Missouri Stake and has held numerous other callings. He is married to Donna Lynn McCutcheon and they have seven children.

SALINA KANSAS STAKE

Covering an expanse of prairie about 220 miles from east to west and 150 miles from the Nebraska border south, the Salina Stake was organized on May 31, 1988 by Elder Dallin H. Oaks of the Council of the Twelve Apostles, with Thomas Robert Coleman as stake president.

The stake participates yearly in the Kansas State Fair and takes pride in the honors won by its youth in fine arts, sports, academics and civic affairs.

THOMAS ROBERT COLEMAN was set apart as stake president when the stake was organized in May 1988. He is a clinical psychologist, a U.S. Army veteran and former member of a forest fire fighting team with 75 parachute jumps. He served in the Andes South Mission, is a former bishop and stake presdient's counselor, and has received Scouting's Silver Beaver Award. He is a native of Bismark, North Dakota and grew up in Glendive, Montana where at age 9, he was the first person to join the Church. He is married to Carolyn Hyer and they have seven children.

SPRINGFIELD MISSOURI STAKE

Documented Latter-day Saint history in southwestern Missouri begins with the organization of a dependent Sunday School in 1915 with John Easton as superintendent, under the direction of the Central States Mission. A Relief Society was organized in 1921 and the Springfield Missouri Branch was established in August of that same year.

The area became part of the Ozark Missouri Stake when it was organized on April 29, 1973 by Elder Spencer W. Kimball, then of the Council of the Twelve Apostles, with C.S. Claybrook as stake president. Soon thereafter the name was changed to the Springfield Missouri Stake. Some territory was taken in 1977 to help form the Joplin Missouri Stake.

G. TIM GOODMAN was set apart as stake president on May 21, 1995. A cattle rancher, he has been a stake president's counselor, bishop, high council member and elders quorum president. He served in the Manitoba, Minnesota Mission. He was born and reared in the Phoenix, Arizona area. He is married to Deborah Lynn Johnson and they have seven children.

SPRINGFIELD MISSOURI SOUTH STAKE

From 1915, when 18 Latter-day Saints began meeting as a dependent Sunday School, Springfield area membership grew steadily until the first stake was organized in the region in 1973. The Ozark Missouri Stake was eventually split to form the Joplin Missouri and Springfield Missouri stakes.

The Springfield South Stake was formed on May 26, 1995, by Elder R. Enzio Busche of the Seventy, with Robert C. Brusman as stake president. Membership growth has accelerated as the area has become the fastest-growing region in Missouri.

STANLEY DALE PETERSEN was set apart as stake president on August 4, 1996. He operates a massage therapy practice and a massage therapy school. He is a former stake president's counselor, high council member, bishop's counselor and young men president. He was born in Mesa, Arizona and grew up in nearby Gilbert, Arizona. He served a mission in Brazil. He is married to Vernene Cluff and they have seven children.

ST. LOUIS MISSOURI STAKE

Parley P. Pratt led a missionary group through St. Louis in 1831 and Joseph Smith traveled through in 1832. The city was an oasis of tolerance for Church members during its early years in Missouri and a stake was established in 1854 to accommodate Latter-day Saints who were gathering for their journey to the Rocky Mountains. The stake was disorganized three years later after most members moved west. Membership growth resumed after Roy G. Oscarson and his family moved to St. Louis in 1945, and he was called as president of the St. Louis Branch when it was established that same year.

The St. Louis Stake was re-established on June 1, 1958 by Elder Mark E. Petersen of the Quorum of the Twelve Apostles, with Brother Oscarson as stake president. Its outgrowth has since helped form all or parts of four other stakes in Missouri and Illinois.

G. RICHARD OSCARSON, a son of Roy Oscarson, was set apart as stake president in February 1989. A retired executive for Edison Brothers Stores Inc, he is currently president of Enterprise Mentors International. He served as president of the Sweden Stockholm Mission and has been a bishop, mission president's counselor, stake president's counselor, high council member, bishop's counselor and elders quorum president. Born in Seattle, Washington and lived there and in California before moving to St. Louis with his family at age 8. He is married to Linda Lochhead and they have six children.

142

ST. LOUIS MISSOURI NORTH STAKE

In a division of the St. Louis Missouri Stake, the St. Louis Missouri North Stake was formed on March 14, 1987, by Dallin H. Oaks of the Quorum of the Twelve Apostles, with Neal C. Lewis as stake president.

The stake shares the St. Louis area's rich Church history and has experienced the same steady membership growth. A new stake center was built in Hazelwood and the first meetings were held there in 1988. It was dedicated in June 1989.

H. KENT MUNSON was set apart as stake president on December 8, 1996. A lawyer, he is a former stake president's counselor, high council member, bishop, bishop's counselor and seminary teacher. He is a native of Loa, Utah and served a mission in Mexico. He is married to Lorrie Rich and they have three children.

ST. LOUIS MISSOURI SOUTH STAKE

The St. Louis South Stake was organized on March 16, 1980, by Elder Mark E. Peterson of the Quorum of the Twelve Apostles, with Verner L. Stromberg Jr. as stake president. It had been part of the St. Louis Missouri Stake and shares that stake's historical heritage.

A new stake center was established in a meetinghouse that had been built on Butler Hill Road in south St. Louis and dedicated by President Spencer W. Kimball on July 2, 1978. An anonymous donor, a nonmember woman, had contributed over $1,000 to its construction. Some of the stake's units were taken to help form the Cape Girardeau Missouri Stake in 1985.

GEORGE DEE BANKHEAD was set apart as stake president on October 29, 1989. An orthodontist, he is a former stake president's counselor, bishop, high council member, bishop's counselor and elders quorum president. He was born in Logan, Utah and reared on a farm in nearby Avon. He is married to Anita Stokes and they have six children.

The Topeka Stake was established on February 28 and 29, 1976, at a conference held in Wichita, Kansas with Vahl W. Boldly as stake president. The stake began with 10 wards and branches that had previously been parts of Wichita Kansas and Kansas City Missouri stakes.

Plans for a new stake center were announced in 1991 and the building was dedicated in 1993. By June 1996, the stake's membership had grown to 3,458. Historical highlights have included a regional conference at Wichita in June 1978, presided over by President Spencer W. Kimball, and a Solemn Assembly at Kansas City, also presided over by President Kimball, in February 1977.

DENNIS HANKS KARPOWITZ was set apart as stake president on November 20, 1994. He is chairman of the Department of Psychology at the University of Kansas. His former Church callings include stake president's counselor, bishop, stake executive secretary, high council member and Sunday School president. He served a mission in Berlin, Germany. Born and reared in Salt Lake City, he is married to Dorothy Diane Carpenter and they have six children.

Made in the USA
Lexington, KY
18 January 2018